T0302973

Improving the Availability and Affordability of Pandemic Risk Insurance

Projected Performance of Proposed Programs

LLOYD DIXON, JAMIE MORIKAWA

Supported by the Kenneth R. Feinberg Center for Catastrophic Risk Management and Compensation Advisory Board and the American Property Casualty Insurance Association

RAND

Kenneth R. Feinberg Center for Catastrophic Risk Management and Compensation

For more information on this publication, visit **www.rand.org/t/RRA1223-1**.

About RAND

The RAND Corporation is a research organization that develops solutions to public policy challenges to help make communities throughout the world safer and more secure, healthier and more prosperous. RAND is nonprofit, nonpartisan, and committed to the public interest. To learn more about RAND, visit www.rand.org.

Research Integrity

Our mission to help improve policy and decisionmaking through research and analysis is enabled through our core values of quality and objectivity and our unwavering commitment to the highest level of integrity and ethical behavior. To help ensure our research and analysis are rigorous, objective, and nonpartisan, we subject our research publications to a robust and exacting quality-assurance process; avoid both the appearance and reality of financial and other conflicts of interest through staff training, project screening, and a policy of mandatory disclosure; and pursue transparency in our research engagements through our commitment to the open publication of our research findings and recommendations, disclosure of the source of funding of published research, and policies to ensure intellectual independence. For more information, visit www.rand.org/about/principles.

RAND's publications do not necessarily reflect the opinions of its research clients and sponsors.

Published by the RAND Corporation, Santa Monica, Calif.

Library of Congress Cataloging-in-Publication Data is available for this publication.

ISBN: 978-1-9774-0707-8

Cover: Design by Rick Penn-Kraus. Photos: anyaberkut/Getty Images/iStockphoto (man with umbrella); BlackJack3D/Getty Images/iStockphoto (coronavirus).

About This Report

Given the closures and other restrictions on business activity during the COVID-19 pandemic, stakeholders have developed several proposals for an insurance-based program to provide businesses with the resources needed to maintain payroll and benefits and to cover the ongoing operating expenses necessary to survive. This report describes the distinguishing features of the most-visible proposals and develops a quantitative model that shows their potential consequences. Proposed programs are evaluated in terms of the proportion of revenue decline replaced (efficacy), efficiency, affordability, the risk borne by commercial insurers, expected annual government net outlays, and the amount of subsidy provided to policyholders. The analysis should be useful to members of Congress, congressional staff, insurers, and policyholders as they consider whether to support the creation of a pandemic risk insurance program and how such a program can be best designed.

The RAND Kenneth R. Feinberg Center for Catastrophic Risk Management and Compensation

The Feinberg Center seeks to identify and promote laws, programs, and institutions that reduce the adverse social and economic effects of natural and manmade catastrophes by improving incentives to reduce future losses; providing just compensation to those suffering losses while appropriately allocating liability to responsible parties; helping affected individuals, businesses, and communities to recover quickly; and avoiding unnecessary legal, administrative, and other transaction costs.

Questions or comments about this report should be sent to the project leader, Lloyd Dixon (dixon@rand.org). For more information about the Feinberg Center, see www.rand.org/ccrmc or contact the director at ccrmc@rand.org.

Funding

Funding for this research was provided by the generous contributions of the RAND Kenneth R. Feinberg Center for Catastrophic Risk Management and Compensation Advisory Board and, in part, by a contribution to the center by the American Property Casualty Insurance Association.

Acknowledgments

This report was improved by comments, information, and expertise provided by many people. We would like to thank staff at the American Property Casualty Insurance Association for directing us to useful data sources, discussing assumptions they have used in projecting the impacts of their proposed Business Continuity Protection Program, and providing insurance industry financial statistics. The Reinsurance Association of America provided helpful information on modeling approaches and data. Chubb provided insight into the structure and modeling of its proposed program. Charles Landgraf at Arnold and Porter helped us better understand and describe the Business Continuity Coalition proposal. Davide Priebe at Guy Carpenter provided valuable insights into the strengths and weakness of different approaches.

Constructive peer reviews of the draft report were provided by Michael Dworsky at the RAND Corporation and Jason Schupp at the Center for Better Insurance. Very helpful comments were also provided by AIG, Liberty Mutual, State Farm, and Travelers. Paul Steinberg at RAND improved the flow and clarity of the exposition, and Rebecca Fowler skillfully edited the document.

Contents

Figures and Tables

Figures

Tables

Summary

The COVID-19 pandemic led to a substantial drop in U.S. economic activity in 2020. Government stay-at-home orders, restrictions on business activities, and consumer concerns about potential exposure to the virus caused unemployment rates to rise and put many businesses in financial jeopardy. Businesses often purchase business interruption coverage that covers loss of revenue due to fires and other perils, but policies typically require that the interruption be due to physical damage at the insured property, and, in recent years, the policies have excluded loss due to contagious diseases. As a result, insurers have held that in most cases they are not obligated to cover the enormous business interruption losses caused by COVID-19.

Now, insurers, insurance industry trade groups, policyholder groups, and Congress have developed proposals that would enhance the role that insurance plays in providing businesses with the resources they need to maintain payroll and benefits and cover ongoing operating expenses during an outbreak. The most visible proposals are the following:

- **The Business Continuity Protection Program (BCPP)**—proposed by the American Property Casualty Insurance Association, the National Association of Mutual Insurance Companies, and the Independent Insurance Agents and Brokers of America—provides payroll, benefits, and expense support to the private sector in the event of a declared public health emergency.
- **Chubb's Pandemic Business Interruption Program** has two parts: the **Pandemic Business Expense Insurance Program**, which is open to small and medium-sized firms (firms with 500 or fewer employees), and the **Pandemic Business Interruption Reinsurance program (Pandemic Re)**, which is open to firms with more than 500 employees.
- **The Zurich Preliminary Pandemic Proposal** proposes a flexible program that allows insurers to choose how much risk to bear.
- **The Pandemic Risk Insurance Act of 2020 (PRIA),** introduced by Representative Carolyn Maloney in May 2020, seeks to establish a Pandemic Risk Reinsurance Program modeled on the federal Terrorism Risk Insurance Program.
- **The Business Continuity Coalition (BCC)** proposal would make coverage for pandemic-related losses available in a broader range of insurance policies than

other proposals. The BCC is composed of insurance policyholders from across the U.S. economy.

Objectives and Approach

This report seeks to inform the discussion of the benefits and drawbacks of the five proposals for expanding insurance for revenue declines due to pandemic-induced business closures or restrictions on economic activity by addressing the following research questions:

- What are the distinguishing features of the most visible proposals for a pandemic risk insurance program?
- How will these programs perform in terms of specific key dimensions: efficacy, efficiency, affordability, risk borne by commercial insurers, government net outlays, and the extent of policyholder subsidies?

To address these questions, we first identified the most-visible proposals and compared their key features. We then developed a high-level, quantitative model to project the key outcomes for each of the proposals. The model is based on a number of underlying parameters, and we reviewed economic and insurance literature and data to develop reasonable values for each. We also consulted with experts about what values would be reasonable. The model uses several simplifying assumptions for each program. In some cases, these assumptions were necessary because the program proposal is silent on the particular issue. In others, we made assumptions to simplify comparisons across programs. For example, the coverages provided by many of the proposals are similar but not identical. We standardized the coverage to allow use of a demand function that enables us to compare take-up rates across programs. Thus, we project outcomes for insurance programs that are similar, but not identical, to those proposed. Harmonizing some aspects of the proposals allows us to better highlight the strengths and weaknesses of the different approaches. For this study, we modeled programs motivated by the BCPP, Chubb, and PRIA programs. The results of these models give insights into the performance of the Zurich and BCC programs, which we did not separately model. For each modeled program, we projected outcomes in a base case and then examined the sensitivity of the results to variation of the underlying parameters over plausible ranges. The modeled programs were evaluated in terms of efficacy, efficiency, affordability, risk borne by commercial insurers, expected annual government net outlays, and policyholder subsidy.

Results

The relative performance of the modeled programs under the base-case parameter assumptions is summarized in Table S.1. In the base case, insurers use a five-year pandemic return period in pricing the risk that they bear. Such a return period would be most relevant in the first years after an insurance program is signed into law, and the law applies to losses due to COVID-19 and its variants.

For small and medium-sized firms, the BCPP approach performs best in terms of affordability, efficacy, and efficiency. The PRIA approach does the best in terms of expected annual net government outlays and policyholder subsidy. It also does best in terms of risk borne by commercial insurers, assuming that *best* in this context means the most risk borne by commercial insurers. For large firms, the BCPP approach again performs best in terms of affordability, efficacy, and efficiency. The PRIA approach still transfers the most risk to commercial insurers, but the Chubb approach now generates the lowest expected annual government net outlays and policyholder subsidy. A summary of the findings on each metric follows.

Affordability

The greater efficiency of the BCPP approach and the ability of the government to spread risk over a longer period than the private sector can results in the BCPP's lower premium (Figure S.1). Although the $442 premium projected for small and medium-sized firms in the BCPP approach seems modest, it remains to be seen whether 65 percent of firms would buy coverage at this rate, as assumed in the base case. Very rough calculations suggest that premiums at this level could increase the cost of commercial multiple peril policies on the order of 4.4 to 8.8 percent. Some firms may be reluctant

Table S.1
Ranking of Modeled Programs by Program Metric at Base-Case Parameter Values

	Small and Medium-Sized Firms			Large Firms		
Program Metric	BCPP Approach	Chubb Approach	PRIA Approach	BCPP Approach	Chubb Approach	PRIA Approach
Affordability	Most	Mid	Least	Most	Least	Mid
Efficacy	Highest	Mid	Lowest	Highest	Lowest	Mid
Efficiency	Highest	Mid	Lowest	Highest	Mid	Lowest
Risk borne by commercial insurers	Least	Mid	Most	Least	Mid	Most
Expected annual net government outlays	Highest	Mid	Lowest	Highest	Lowest	Mid
Policyholder subsidy	Most	Mid	Least	Most	Least	Mid

NOTE: Shading indicates the program that performs best on the metric.

Figure S.1
Annual Premium in Base-Case Projection

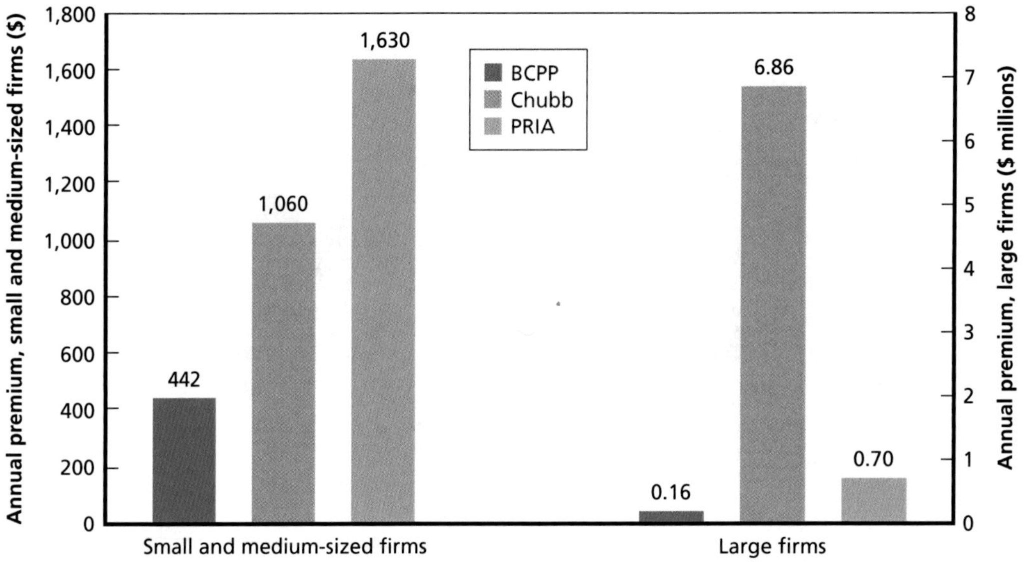

to purchase coverage at these rates, remembering the large government-funded Paycheck Protection Program (PPP) in the current pandemic.

The premiums for large firms are comparable to those for small firms in the BCPP and PRIA approaches when normalized by payroll (premium per $1,000 payroll). Due to the market-based rate charged for the risk borne by the government, the premium charged by Chubb's Pandemic Re is projected to be much higher ($6.86 million per firm) than in the other two approaches.

Efficacy

None of the programs does a particularly good job in terms of the percentage of losses reimbursed over a 12-month pandemic (efficacy). This is largely because of the moderate to low take-up rates and the 20 percent policyholder co-pay (Figure S.2). The BCPP approach does best because its lower premium results in the highest take-up rate. Take-up and the percentage of losses reimbursed for the large firms in Chubb's Pandemic Re approach are particularly low. Large firms presumably have a better ability to weather revenue declines than smaller firms, but the fact remains that they account for 60 percent of payroll at firms with employees, and their financial health will have important consequences for overall employment levels during a pandemic.

Efficiency

Program efficiency is the ratio of claim payment to overall program costs and driven by general and selling expenses, loss adjustment expenses, and private-sector capital

Figure S.2
Take-Up Rate in Base-Case Projection

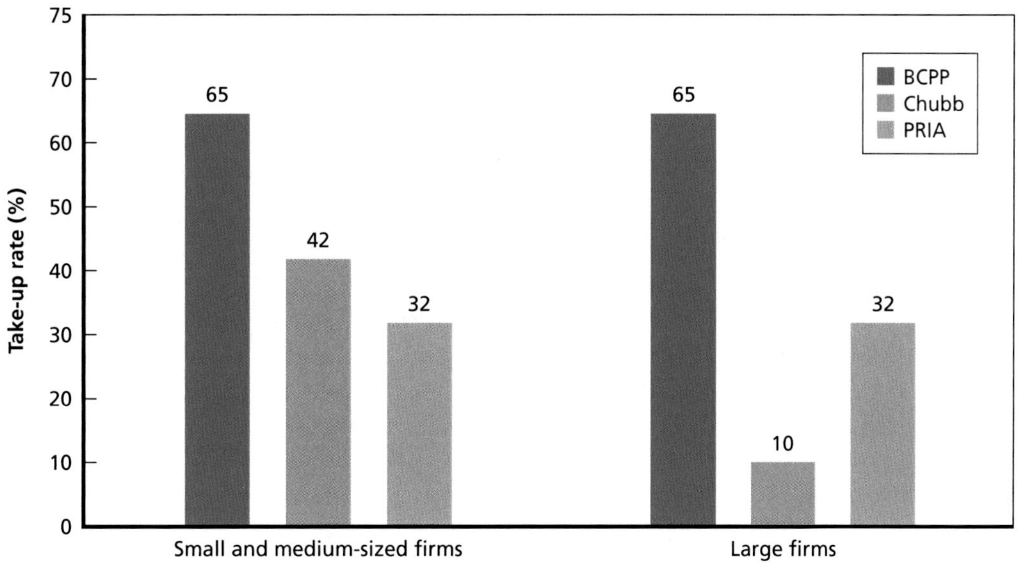

costs. BCPP does best on this metric partly because it relies on parametric policies to reduce costs and to address the practical problem of simultaneously adjusting an enormous number of claims.[1] BCPP also fares best in part because it does not require insurers to hold capital to protect against solvency risk. The cost of such capital is the cost of transferring risk from the public to commercial insurers. Higher capital costs reduce efficiency but are associated with lower government outlays should an event occur and with other potential benefits that come with greater private-sector skin in the game. These other potential benefits include greater attention to fraudulent claims, as well as the development of the expertise and experience needed to grow the private sector's ability to write pandemic risk. When deciding whether to proceed with a pandemic risk insurance program, program efficiency should be compared with that of other approaches, such as the PPP. We found that the efficiency of the BCPP approach compares favorably to the administrative costs of the PPP, but unless pandemic return periods are short, efficiencies of the other program do not compare so favorably.

---

[1] Payment by a parametric insurance policy is triggered by a metric or index that is easy to determine rather than property damage or other loss suffered by the insured. In the context of pandemic risk insurance, payment would be triggered following a government declaration of a public health emergency and restricted to firms in the geographic area and industries identified in the closure order. Such a parametric trigger would avoid the need for the traditional claims adjustment process associated with indemnity policies.

Risk Borne by Commercial Insurers

The amount of risk borne by commercial insurers is highest in PRIA, but, reflecting the difficulty of insuring pandemic risk, it is not particularly high in any of the programs. Chubb proposes that the insurer risk share double over time, but even so, it will remain modest. One advantage of the insurer deductible in the PRIA approach is that the share of losses borne by insurers would be higher in smaller or better-contained pandemics. The capital insurers' need to hedge solvency risk is not large relative to industry surplus for the Chubb and PRIA approaches (3.8 percent of an estimated $325 billion for commercial lines), but further analysis is required to determine how difficult it would be for the industry to raise this amount of capital.

Expected Annual Government Net Outlays and Policyholder Subsidy

Illustrating the usual trade-off between affordability and government cost, the BCPP approach does best on affordability but worst on expected government annual net outlays and policyholder subsidy. Expected annual government net outlays depend on what the pandemic return period (as opposed to the return period used by insurers in setting premiums) turns out to be. There is a great deal of uncertainty regarding this return period, and Figure S.3 plots expected annual government net outlays for different return periods. As can be seen, expected annual net outlays are lowest for the

Figure S.3
Expected Annual Government Net Outlays at Base-Case Parameter Values

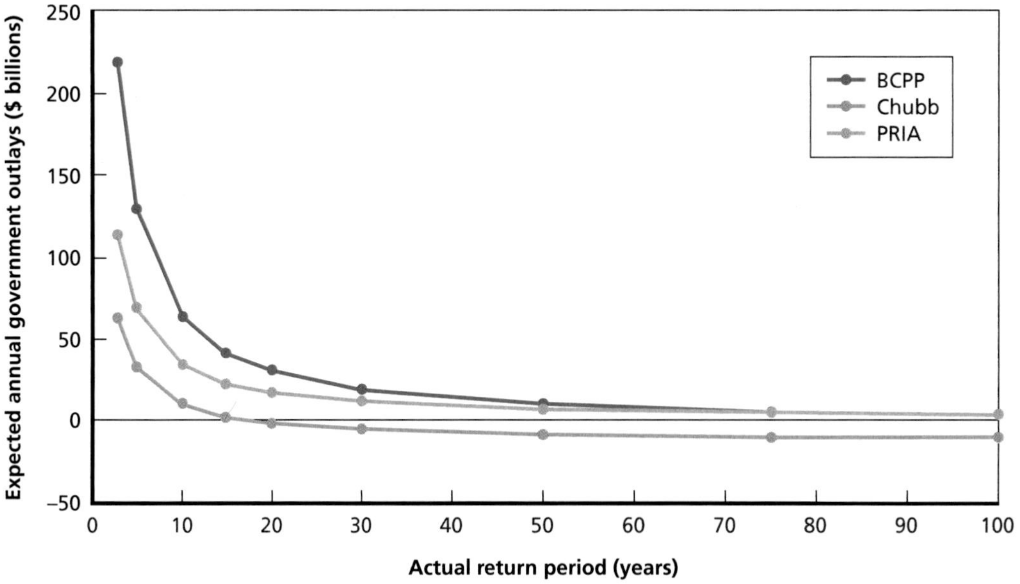

Chubb approach, with government generating a surplus in the base case if the return period turns out to be approximately ten years longer than the five-year return period insurers use in setting premiums.

Our measure of government net outlays is only the direct revenues and outlays of the program. Indirect costs, such as an increased demand for government assistance during an event when there is limited insurance coverage, should also be considered when assessing the full effect of a pandemic insurance program on overall government outlays. Such an analysis was beyond the scope of this study, but the amount of risk borne by commercial insurers is likely a better indicator of overall net government outlays than direct government outlays through the pandemic insurance program.

Projected outcomes are sensitive to several underlying model parameters about which there is considerable uncertainly. In particular, the pandemic return period that insurers use in pricing coverage has an important impact on expected premium and take-up in the Chubb and PRIA approaches. If the proposed programs do not apply to COVID-19 and its variants, a longer return period than the five years used in the base case might be a more accurate expectation of insurer behavior. When the return period used by insurers in setting prices is 30 years, the projected premiums for small and medium-sized firms is similar in all three programs (Figure S.4). The premium for large firms remains substantially higher in the Chubb approach than in the other two approaches.

Figure S.4
Annual Premium When Insurers Use 30-Year Return Period in Setting Prices and Other Parameters Remain at Base-Case Values

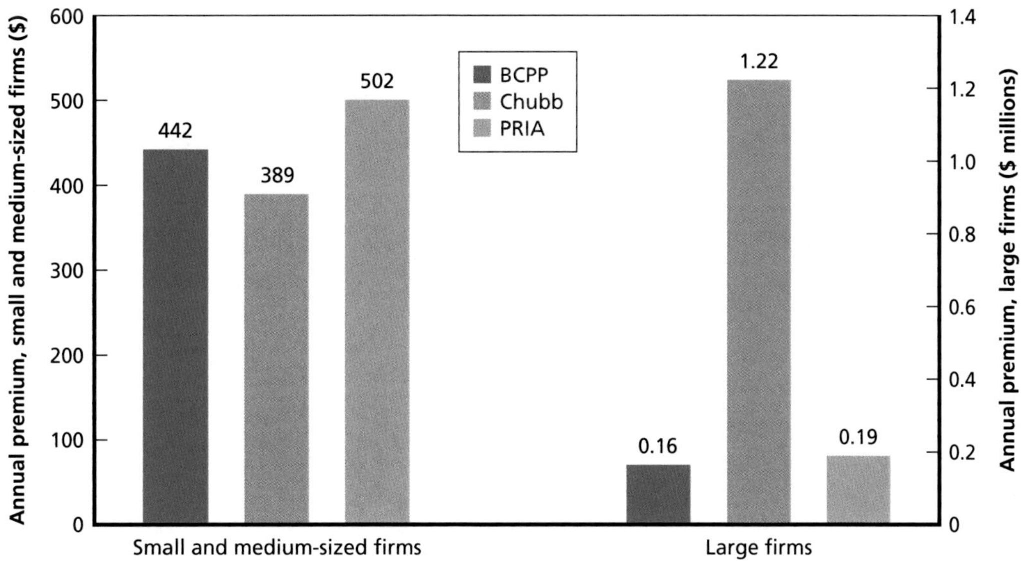

As apparent from Table S.1, no program as currently proposed dominates the others on all the performance metrics. Rather, each has advantages and disadvantages in terms of the performance metrics of concern.

Limitations

This analysis provides information useful to assessing the advantages and disadvantages of different approaches for improving the availability and affordability of pandemic risk insurance. However, it does not seek to evaluate and compare the full range of policy options for addressing pandemic losses. Such a policy analysis would systematically compare the advantages and disadvantages of an insurance-based approach with a government-based approach, such as the PPP. That analysis would also take a more comprehensive view of some of the outcome measures used in this analysis. For example, in this report, we projected government net outlays directly through the proposed programs, but a more comprehensive analysis would include the indirect effects of the program on other government outlays.

The various proposals that we have examined contain several important gaps that remain to be filled—for example,

- whether and how the parametric trigger would address firms either subject to a partial shutdown order or that experience substantial revenue decline but are not subject to a closure order
- whether policies backed by PRIA would provide coverage for pandemic losses when the underlying business interruption policies require physical damage to the insured property
- whether parametric policies would result in some firms receiving more compensation than they need and others less (basis risk).

In this analysis, we have in effect assumed that gaps are filled, thereby resulting in the right amount of assistance getting to the right firms, but additional work is needed to flesh out the proposals to deal with these and other gaps and to determine the extent to which unaddressed issues can be resolved.

Abbreviations

B	billions
BCC	Business Continuity Coalition
BCPP	Business Continuity Protection Program
BEIP	Business Expense Insurance Program (Chubb)
BI	business interruption
BOP	business owner policy
COVID-19	coronavirus disease 2019
G&SE	general and selling expenses
GDP	gross domestic product
LAE	loss adjustment expenses
M	millions
NAIC	National Association of Insurance Commissioners
P&C	property and casualty
Pandemic Re	Pandemic Reinsurance Program (Chubb)
PPP	Paycheck Protection Program
PRIA	Pandemic Risk Insurance Act of 2020
T	trillions
TRIP	Terrorism Risk Insurance Program
ZPPP	Zurich Preliminary Pandemic Program

CHAPTER ONE

Introduction

The COVID-19 pandemic led to a substantial drop in U.S. economic activity in the first part of 2020. Government stay-at-home orders, restrictions on business activities, and consumer concerns about potential exposure to the virus caused unemployment rates to rise and put many businesses in financial jeopardy. Businesses often purchase business interruption (BI) coverage for loss of revenue because of fires and other perils, but policies typically require that the interruption was due to physical damage at the insured property, and, in recent years, the policies have excluded loss due to contagious diseases. As a result, insurers have held that in most cases they are not obligated to cover the enormous BI closures caused by COVID-19.[1]

Using an insurance approach to address pandemic risk has several advantages. These include the ability to define benefits and a benefit distribution mechanism in advance rather than rely on a hastily crafted government program. Also, an insurance approach can leverage the deep capabilities of the commercial insurance industry to place policies and to adjust claims. Moreover, insurance can transfer some risk to the private sector.[2]

However, pandemic risk also creates a number of challenges for the private sector. The global reach of pandemics limits the ability of insurers to diversify and spread risk. As in the case of terrorism, pandemic impacts are very much determined by government decisions that make it difficult to estimate potential losses or price policies. In the case of pandemics, these decisions involve how broadly to restrict business and social activity.[3] As a result, commercial insurers have little interest in providing coverage for

---

[1] Appendix A provides an overview of BI policies.

[2] In other settings, insurance can create incentives to reduce risk by providing premium reductions to policyholders that adopt risk mitigation measures. It is not obvious, however, whether insurance can create similar incentives to mitigate pandemic risk. As an example, consider a mitigation measure that would reduce seating capacity in a restaurant during an outbreak. Such a measure would increase revenue loss, justifying an increase, not decrease, in premium.

[3] For a discussion of the insurability challenges posed by pandemics, see Hartwig, Robert, Greg Niehaus, and Joseph Qiu, "Insurance for Economic Losses Caused by Pandemics," *Geneva Risk and Insurance Review*, Vol. 45, 2020.

pandemic-induced business closures or restrictions on business activity, as evidenced by the policy exclusions put in place before the COVID-19 outbreak and moves by insurers to broaden these exclusions in the wake of COVID-19.

Insurers, insurance industry trade groups, policyholder groups, and Congress have developed proposals that would enhance the role that insurance plays in providing businesses with the resources they need to maintain payroll and benefits and to cover the ongoing operating expenses during an outbreak. Some of these approaches are motivated by the federal Terrorism Risk Insurance Program (TRIP) that was adopted following the 9/11 attacks in response to the lack of insurance coverage for terrorism events. Other approaches are shaped by the particular features of pandemic risk.

Research Questions and Study Approach

This report seeks to inform the discussion of the benefits and drawbacks of the different approaches for expanding insurance for pandemic-induced business closures or restrictions on business activity by addressing the following research questions:

- What are the distinguishing features of the most-visible proposals for a pandemic risk insurance program?
- How will these programs perform in terms of specific key dimensions: efficacy, efficiency, affordability, risk borne by commercial insurers, and the extent of policyholder subsidies?

Although this report will compare, to some extent, an insurance-based approach for addressing losses due to pandemics with an approach based on government programs, such as the Paycheck Protection Program (PPP), it does not seek to evaluate and compare the full range of policy approaches for addressing pandemic losses. Rather, it seeks to inform the debate on how society can best address pandemic risk by comparing the different insurance-related approaches and predict how they might perform under a range of assumptions.

To address these research questions, we first identified the most-visible proposals and compared their key features. We then developed a high-level, quantitative model to project the key outcomes for each of the proposals. This model is based on a number of underlying parameters, and we reviewed economic and insurance literature and data to develop reasonable values for these parameters. We also consulted with experts in the field about what values would be reasonable.[4] For each program, we projected out-

---

[4] The experts we consulted had considerable knowledge about the cost components of and pricing practices for insurance policies or about the provisions of proposed pandemic risk insurance programs. Interviews followed a semistructured, open-ended format and were conducted via Microsoft Teams between November 2020 and April 2021.

comes in a base case and then examined the sensitivity of the results to variation of the parameters over plausible ranges.

Report Organization

Chapter Two describes five pandemic insurance programs: three proposed by insurers or insurance industry associations, one proposed by a coalition of business policyholders, and one proposed by members of Congress. Chapter Three describes the modeling approach and the parameters used in the projections, while Chapter Four presents and discusses the projected outcomes for the base-case set of parameter values. Chapter Five examines the sensitivity of the results to changes in parameter values, and concluding comments are provided in Chapter Six. The provisions of a typical BI insurance policy are described in Appendix A. The equations that underlie the pandemic risk insurance model that we developed are presented in Appendix B. Appendix C provides an example of how insurance payments might be determined when a business is partially, as opposed to fully, shut down. Insurance industry data on general and selling expenses (G&SE) and loss adjustment expenses (LAE) by property and casualty (P&C) insurance line are provided in Appendix D.

CHAPTER TWO

Overview of Proposed Programs

In this chapter, we compare and contrast five of the most-visible proposals for providing business firms with the support they need to cover payroll, benefits, and ongoing operating expenses during the economic disruption caused by a pandemic. Three of these proposals have been offered by insurers or insurance industry groups, one has been offered by a policyholder group, and the final has been introduced as congressional legislation. In each case, we describe the policy offered to businesses (the policy features) and the features of the program provided to participating insurers (the program features). Businesses pay a premium to insurers for the coverage, and, in some cases, insurers pass on part of this premium to the federal government for the risk it bears. In the context of the proposed pandemic risk insurance programs, the risk sharing provided by the government is sometimes referred to as *reinsurance* and sometimes as a *government backstop*.[1] Insurers might or might not pay a premium for this coverage.

Proposal 1: Business Continuity Protection Program

The Business Continuity Protection Program (BCPP)—proposed by the American Property Casualty Insurance Association, the National Association of Mutual Insurance Companies, and the Independent Insurance Agents and Brokers of America—provides payroll, benefits, and support for ongoing operating expenses to the private sector in the event of a declared public health emergency.[2] This revenue replacement assistance would be available through state-regulated insurance entities that voluntarily participate in the BCPP.

---

1 *Reinsurance* refers insurance purchased by primary insurers from other insurers (the reinsurers). Primary insurers are insurers that write policies for the end customer—whether a business or an individual.

2 This description of the BCPP is based on American Property Casualty Insurance Association, Independent Insurance Agents and Brokers of America, Inc., and National Association of Mutual Insurance Companies, *Business Continuity Protection Program*, updated September 2020.

Policy Features

The policy offered to businesses would provide up to three months of payroll, benefits, and ongoing operating expenses and would be available to all for-profit and nonprofit businesses ("Policy Features" section of Table 2.1). The revenue losses could occur anytime during the typical one-year policy period, meaning that a total of three times the monthly payroll, benefits, and ongoing operating expenses could be paid over the course of the policy. Purchase would be voluntary, although a strong opt-out would be required: Firms declining coverage would have to acknowledge in writing that they would be ineligible for benefits if a pandemic-related business closure occurs.

There is no waiting period before payments begin, and policyholders could select the policyholder co-pay, subject to a 20 percent minimum. Payment would automatically be triggered following a government declaration of a public health emergency and restricted to firms in the geographic area and industries identified in the closure order. Such a parametric trigger would avoid the need for the traditional claims adjustment process associated with indemnity policies.

Several questions remain about how the trigger would work in practice. First, the proposal does not discuss whether payments would be triggered for firms that suffer revenue declines but are not directly subject to a shutdown order. For example, would payments be provided to a travel agency that can operate remotely but whose business drops because hotels are closed?

Second, the proposal also does not discuss how partial shutdowns would be handled. When a business completely shuts down and its revenue falls to zero, a claim payment equal to payroll, benefits, and ongoing operating costs would allow the firm to maintain payroll and survive until the policy limit is reached. For a policy limit equal to three months of preshutdown payroll, benefits, and ongoing operating expenses, the coverage would last for three months under a complete shutdown. Claim payments would not cover preshutdown profits or the costs that the firm can readily reduce (variable costs). In a partial shutdown (for example, restaurants that are able to operate at 25 percent seating capacity and provide takeout service), revenue would not fall to zero. The BCPP proposal does not discuss how claim payment would be adjusted if this were the case. If the same claim payment were made as in a full shutdown, the firms would likely need to return some of the payment if the goal is to maintain payroll, benefits, and ongoing expenses but not to reimburse foregone profits. Appendix B describes how much would have to be returned under various scenarios. The analysis shows that firms would have to consider preshutdown profits and their success in reducing variable costs during the shutdown when determining how much of the parametric payment to return or reserve for future use. Whether and how such a process would be implemented remains to be specified.[3]

---

[3] The proposal also does not address some of the regulatory issues associated with parametric insurance policies. Under some configurations, parametric policies might be considered financial derivatives and therefore might be

Program Features

Insurer participation in the program is voluntary, but participating insurers would be required to offer the pandemic coverage to all firms that purchase specified lines of insurance. Insurers would be reimbursed for payments by the federal government. Thus, there is no insurer deductible or co-pay. The federal government would also reimburse participating insurers for the costs associated with selling policies and operating the program (G&SE), as well as for LAE. The BCPP leverages the capacity of commercial insurers to issue policies, collect premiums, and pay claims, but all loss payments and program costs would be funded by the federal government.

The BCPP proposes that the premium paid by policyholders be set at a percentage of policyholder revenue that does not vary over firm size or industry. The premium would be set "to ensure widespread take-up," but it would be left to the government to determine what fraction of expected program costs would be recovered through the policyholder premium.[4]

As with the policy features of the BCPP proposal, some aspects of program features are not fully fleshed out. For example, insurer participation in the program is voluntary, and it is not clear what would happen to businesses whose insurers decided not to participate in the program. Would such business be able to buy coverage from other insurers, and, if so, how might the cost of the policy be affected? It might be more expensive for an insurer to set up coverage with a new policyholder than to add pandemic coverage on to an existing policy

Proposal 2: Chubb Pandemic Business Interruption Program

Chubb's Pandemic Business Interruption Program has two parts. Part I, the pandemic Business Expense Insurance Program (BEIP), is open to small and medium-sized firms, which are firms with 500 or fewer employees. Part II, the Pandemic Business Interruption Reinsurance program (Pandemic Re), is open to firms with more than 500 employees. We describe each program in turn.[5]

Chubb Business Expense Insurance Program

Policy Features

The BEIP provides coverage similar to the BCPP in many respects (as shown in Table 2.1). Payroll and expenses are covered (the proposal is silent on benefits) for up to three months, a simple parametric structure provides for accelerated claim payments,

---

subject to oversight by the Commodities Futures Trading Commission, as opposed to state insurance regulators. Consideration of such issues is beyond the scope of this analysis.

[4] American Property Casualty Insurance Association, Independent Insurance Agents and Brokers of America, Inc., and National Association of Mutual Insurance Companies, 2020, p. 3.

[5] This description of the Chubb program is based on Chubb, *Pandemic Business Interruption Program*, Warren, N.J., July 8, 2020.

Table 2.1
Features of Proposed Pandemic Risk Insurance Programs

Attribute	Business Continuity Protection Program (BCPP)	Chubb Business Expense Insurance Program (BEIP)	Chubb Pandemic Business Interruption Reinsurance Program (Pandemic Re)	Zurich Preliminary Pandemic Program (ZPPP)	Pandemic Risk Insurance Act (PRIA)	Business Continuity Coalition (BCC) Program
Policy Features						
Firms eligible[a]	All firms	Firms with ≤500 employees	Firms with >500 employees	Firms eligible[a]	All firms	All firms
Losses covered	Payroll, benefits, and ongoing expenses	Payroll and ongoing expenses	Payroll and ongoing expenses	Payroll, benefits, and ongoing expenses	Payroll, benefits, ongoing expenses, event cancellation	Payroll and fixed costs for a nondamage parametric BI policy; same coverage that is provided for other perils in standard P&C policies
Policyholder deductible	No waiting period	14-day waiting period	30-day waiting period (or longer, as desired)	Policyholder can select waiting period	Same as underlying BI policy	None for parametric policy; same as underlying P&C policies for other coverages
Policyholder co-pay	Policyholder choice with 20% minimum	None specified	None specified	20%	Same as underlying BI policy	None for parametric policy; same as underlying P&C policies for other coverage
Policy limit	3 months of payroll, benefits, and ongoing expenses	3 months of payroll, benefits, and ongoing expenses	3 months of payroll, benefits, and ongoing expenses capped at $50M per firm	3 months of payroll, benefits, and expenses, capped at $20M per month for large firms ($60M over 3 months)	Same as underlying BI policy	90 days of payroll and fixed costs for parametric BI policy, same as underlying P&C policies for other coverage
Claim payment mechanism	Parametric	Parametric	Indemnity	Parametric with policyholder required to self-certify losses	Indemnity	Parametric and indemnity

Table 2.1—Continued

Attribute	Business Continuity Protection Program (BCPP)	Chubb Business Expense Insurance Program (BEIP)	Chubb Pandemic Business Interruption Reinsurance Program (Pandemic Re)	Zurich Preliminary Pandemic Program (ZPPP)	Pandemic Risk Insurance Act (PRIA)	Business Continuity Coalition (BCC) Program
Policyholder purchase requirement	Voluntary with strong opt-out	Mandatory or voluntary with strong opt out	Voluntary	Voluntary	Voluntary	Voluntary
Program Features						
Insurer participation requirement	Voluntary	Voluntary	Voluntary	Mandatory	Voluntary	Mandatory
Insurer offer requirement	Participating insurers required to offer to all policyholders who purchase covered lines of commercial insurance	Mandatory offer	Voluntary offer	Mandatory offer to policyholders with fixed property coverage	Mandatory to policyholders who purchase business interruption coverage	Mandatory to businesses with P&C insurance
Program limit	None	$750B	$400B	No limit specified	$750B	No limit
Insurer deductible	$0	$0	$0	$0	5% of direct earned premium in specified lines	$0
Insurer co-pay	0%	6% up to $250B (rising to 12% over 20 years); 0% above $250B	5% up to $300B for first 5 years (rising to 10% by year 10); 0% above $300B	0%, 5%, or 10%; insurers can assign individual policies to any pool	5% of losses above insurer deductible up to $750B	5%
Government charge for backstop	Premium set to ensure widespread take-up	None	Market rate	Below market rate; amount of premium ceded to government depends on pool chosen	None	None during first 5 years; following economic recovery period, government has authority to charge for backstop

Table 2.1—Continued

Attribute	Business Continuity Protection Program (BCPP)	Chubb Business Expense Insurance Program (BEIP)	Chubb Pandemic Business Interruption Reinsurance Program (Pandemic Re)	Zurich Preliminary Pandemic Program (ZPPP)	Pandemic Risk Insurance Act (PRIA)	Business Continuity Coalition (BCC) Program
Source of payment for insurer expenses	Government will pay fee for insurer G&SE and LAE	Premium covers G&SE and LAE	Included in premium; 3% for broker 5–7% for insurer administrative fee; claim handling fee not specified; Pandemic Re administrative and operating fee 0.25% of written premium	Government pays commission to insurers that is 25–30% of premium ceded to government depending on pool chosen	Included in premium	Not discussed
Premium	Based on % of policyholder revenue; uniform across all firms; set to promote widespread take-up	Expected to be small relative to a firm's overall insurance expenses	Both insurers and government are paid an appropriate risk-adjusted price for pandemic cover	Government sets premium with target of 2% rate on line for <500 employees and 3% rate on line for ≥500 employees	Not discussed	Not discussed
Expected take-up rate	Not discussed	90%	30%	Varies by industry (90% for accommodations and food services, 30% for utilities); 65% economy-wide	Not discussed	Not discussed

SOURCES: Author summary based on American Property Casualty Insurance Association, Independent Insurance Agents and Brokers of America, Inc., and National Association of Mutual Insurance Companies, 2020; Chubb, 2020; Zurich, *Zurich's Draft Concept for Facilitating Pandemic Protection*, Los Angeles, Calif., December 7, 2020; U.S. House of Representatives, Pandemic Risk Insurance Act of 2020, H.R. 7011, May 26, 2020; Business Continuity Coalition, "BCC Proposal: A Proposal from the Policyholder Community," September 2020.

[a] Includes both for-profit and nonprofit firms.

and purchase is voluntary with a strong opt-out. Unlike the BCPP, there is a 14-day waiting period between when business closures or restrictions are announced and coverage begins, but there is no policyholder co-pay.

Program Features

Like the BCPP, insurer participation in the program is voluntary, and insurers choosing to participate must offer coverage to their policyholders. The major difference between the two programs is that, in Chubb's proposal, the commercial insurers bear some risk. In the first year of the program, insurers pay 6 percent of claims up to $250 billion in policyholder losses—a maximum of $15 billion. The federal government pays 100 percent of any additional losses up to $750 billion. The industry exposure rises to 12 percent of the first $250 billion (up to $30 billion) over 20 years.

The BEIP envisions a policyholder premium that covers the risk borne by commercial insurers. Insurers do not pay a premium to the government; thus, the policyholder premium does not include a component that covers the potential payments by the federal government. The BEIP proposal does not specify whether the government would reimburse commercial insurers for G&SE; however, given that there is no indication that the government would pay G&SE, it seems reasonable to assume that Chubb envisions these costs being built into the premium—all of which is kept by insurers. Given the strong opt-out and the subsidized premium, Chubb expects 90 percent of small businesses to participate in the program.

Pandemic Re

The objective of Pandemic Re is to promote a market-oriented program for large businesses. Purchase of coverage by the roughly 20,000 businesses with more than 500 employees is voluntary, with no strong opt-out or requirement that insurers offer coverage to large firms.

Policy Features

The policy again looks similar to those offered by the BCPP and Chubb's BEIP: Payroll and expenses are covered for three months with no policyholder co-pay. In this case, however, there is a 30-day waiting period, or longer if desired, and a $50 million cap on payments per policy. Importantly, traditional loss adjustment techniques are used, which are expected to be much more costly than those needed for parametric policies.

Program Features

Insurers pay 5 percent of insured losses up to $300 billion ($15 billion maximum), and again the government pays 100 percent of additional losses up to an overall program cap of $400 billion (government and commercial insurer claim payments combined).

In contrast to the BCPP and the BEIP, Pandemic Re is a program "in which both the insurance industry *and the government* are paid an appropriate risk-adjusted price for pandemic cover" (italics added).[6] We take this to mean that the policyholder premium should cover (1) the expected loss payments and associated LAE for which commercial insurers are financially responsible, G&SE, and the costs of capital required by commercial insurers to mitigate their solvency risk and (2) the government's expected loss payment and the associated LAE. This approach differs critically from the BEIP and BCPP, which charge insurers no premium for the government backstop. A pandemic return period must be assumed to calculate expected loss and LAE. As will be discussed in Chapter Three, the return period is the inverse of the annual probability that a pandemic occurs. Chubb assumes a 30-year return period (0.033 annual probability) in its proposal.

Proposal 3: Zurich Preliminary Pandemic Proposal

Policy Features

The Zurich Preliminary Pandemic Proposal (ZPPP) is open to firms of all sizes and offers coverage very similar to what is offered by the BCPP and Chubb programs. Like the Chubb proposal, the ZPPP includes a limit on claim payments to large policyholders: $20 million per month or $60 million over three months for large firms, compared with $50 million in Chubb's Pandemic Re proposal.

Program Features

The ZPPP proposes a flexible program (see Table 2.1) that allows insurers to choose how much risk to bear. Depending on how much risk insurers choose to bear, the program can end up looking quite similar to the BCPP. It can also end up looking very similar to the Chubb proposal. As will be discussed further, the ZPPP expects insurers to retain 1 percent of the risk, resulting in a program that is similar to the BCPP. The ZPPP is inspired by the federal crop insurance program, with which Zurich has considerable experience.[7]

Like the BCPP and Chubb proposals, insurers participating in the ZPPP must offer coverage to their customers with fixed property coverage. In contrast to the BCPP and Chubb proposals, insurers are required to participate in the ZPPP.

The main distinguishing feature of the ZPPP is that insurers can select how much risk to bear on a policy-by-policy basis. Insurers can place policies in pools in which 100 percent of the premium and risk are ceded to the government, 95 percent is ceded to the government, or 90 percent is ceded to the government. By allocating across pools, insurers can tailor their portfolios to their risk appetites. One advantage of this approach is that insurers can adjust the risk they retain over time by modifying the

---

[6] Chubb, 2020, p. 4.

[7] This description of Zurich's program is based on Zurich, 2020.

distribution of policies across pools. Zurich projects a very modest insurer risk appetite initially and estimates that 99 percent of the premium and risk would be ceded to the federal government in the first years of the program.

Like the federal crop insurance program, policyholder premiums in the ZPPP are subsidized by the federal government.[8] Zurich does not specify the amount of subsidy but envisions a rate on line of 2 percent for small and medium-sized firms and 3 percent for large firms.[9] This target premium can in principle be used to impute an implied level of subsidy.[10] Insurer G&SE and LAE would be covered in part through a commission on the premium ceded to the pool. The ceding commission starts at 25 percent for the 100 percent pool and rises to 30 percent for the 90 percent pool. The ceding commission structure provides an incentive for insurers to bear more risk. Insurers will also use the premium that they retain to cover G&SE, LAE, and the portion of loss payments for which they are responsible.

Zurich expects take-up to vary by industry, projecting in its program proposal, for example, 90 percent and 30 percent take-up rates for the accommodation and food services sector and utilities sector, respectively. Zurich expects take-up rate to average 65 percent across the economy as a whole.[11]

Proposal 4: Pandemic Risk Insurance Act

Introduced by Representative Carolyn Maloney in May 2020, the Pandemic Risk Insurance Act of 2020 (PRIA) seeks to establish the Pandemic Risk Reinsurance Program modeled on the federal TRIP.[12] PRIA requires participating insurers to make available in all BI policies coverage for losses from public health emergencies declared for infectious disease. All firms are eligible for the policy, and purchase is voluntary.[13] In contrast to TRIP, insurer participation in the program is voluntary.

Policy Features

Participating insurers are required to make available coverage for pandemic-related losses that does not differ materially from that available for events other than public

---

8 The federal subsidy in the federal crop insurance program amounts to approximately two-thirds of the premium.

9 *Rate on line* is premium as a percentage of the amount of coverage provided.

10 Zurich would implement a subsidy by allowing the government to use a longer return period in its determination of premium than would be required by the private sector.

11 The 65 percent economy-wide average is based on our conversations with analysts familiar with the Zurich proposal.

12 U.S. House of Representatives, 2020.

13 See U.S. House of Representatives, 2020.

health emergencies. Coverage limits, waiting periods, and the type of expenses covered can vary across BI policies, and PRIA does not specify the amount and scope of coverage that should be provided. BI coverage typically includes such expenses as utilities and rent and lost profit. However, it might not cover payroll for employees that could easily be laid off and then rehired or replaced (see Appendix A for an overview of typical BI coverage). If this were the case, BI coverage backstopped by PRIA might not be sufficient to maintain prepandemic employment levels. In addition, BI coverage often applies only when there has been physical damage to the insured property. Policies that contain such physical damage requirements might not pay out when the cause of loss is a contagious disease.

Program Features

Turning to PRIA's risk-sharing provisions, insurers bear the first layer of loss (the insurer deductible) and then share losses above the deductible with the federal government. Mirroring TRIP, PRIA's deductible for commercial insurers as a whole is 5 percent of the direct earned premium in specified insurance lines of business. As will be discussed in Chapter Three, the insurer deductible would have been roughly $12 billion in 2019. Insurers then are responsible for 5 percent of losses above the program deductible up to $750 billion in insured losses (the maximum industry exposure is thus roughly $49 billion).

Like the Chubb BEIP, the government does not charge a premium for the risk it bears in the PRIA proposal. Insurers will presumably set the premium to cover their share of loss payments and G&SE and LAE.

Proposal 5: Business Continuity Coalition Program

The Business Continuity Coalition (BCC) program provides more-expansive coverage for pandemic-related loss than the other proposals. The BCC is composed of business insurance policyholders from across the U.S. economy.[14]

Policy Features

Insurers would be required to make available coverage for "insured losses related to covered public health emergencies" in *all* their P&C insurance policies.[15] The BCC's mandatory offer requirement is broader than PRIA's. PRIA applies only to BI insurance, including event cancellation. In contrast, the BCC proposal applies to all P&C policies, including workers' compensation, commercial general liability, directors and

---

[14] Business Continuity Coalition, homepage, undated.

[15] Business Continuity Coalition, "Pandemic Risk Insurance Act Business Continuity Coalition Proposal: Section-by-Section Description," March 2021.

officers liability, excess insurance, and event cancellation (subject to several exceptions). The BCC proposal in addition requires insurers to make available to all their P&C policyholders parametric BI coverage. (Insurers can arrange for such coverage to be made available by an affiliate or a parametric insurance facility in which the insurer participates.) The parametric coverage would not require the incident to cause physical damage at the insured property. This parametric nondamage BI coverage would provide 90 days of fixed costs and payroll and would be triggered by certification of a public health emergency and a closure order for the policyholder's North American Industry Classification System (NAICS) code.

Program Features

Unlike the other proposed programs, all insurers would be required to participate in the BCC program. Insurers would bear 5 percent of the losses and the federal government 95 percent. There would be no cap on government or insurer outlays. Insurers would not be charged a premium for the quota share reinsurance provided by the government during an economic recovery period. The economic recovery period covers the five years following congressional enactment of the program and resets if there is a public health emergency during the five years following enactment.

Discussion

The proposed programs share many features but also differ in important ways. The BCPP, Chubb, and Zurich proposals offer similar coverage for payroll, benefits, and ongoing operating expenses. PRIA takes a different approach by requiring insurers to make coverage available for pandemic-related losses that does not differ materially from that available for perils covered by BI provisions. The BCC proposal goes further by supporting insurance coverage for pandemic losses in other lines, such as event cancellation and directors and officers liability, in addition to providing payroll and operating expenses due to BI.

The proposals leverage the underwriting and claim adjusting capabilities of the private sector but vary in the amount of risk borne by commercial insurers. Commercial insurers bear no risk in the BCPP, and insurers are responsible for up to $30 billion in loss payments in the Chubb proposal (small, medium-sized, and large firms combined) initially, doubling over 20 years. Commercial insurers are potentially responsible for $50 billion in losses under PRIA. However, the private insurer share is not large relative to total insured losses in any of the proposals. An attractive feature of the Zurich proposal is that insurers can adjust the risk they retain over time by modifying the distribution of policies across pools.

To reduce the costs of simultaneously adjusting a large number of claims, all but one of the proposals rely at least in part on a parametric trigger. The Chubb proposal takes a hybrid approach, using a parametric trigger for the vast majority of firms with employees that have 500 or fewer employees (discussed further in the following chapter) and an indemnity approach for the relatively few firms with more than 500 employees. PRIA is the only proposal that does not specifically call for the use of a parametric policy, but insurers are presumably free to write policies with parametric triggers if they choose to do so.

Premiums are subsidized either explicitly or implicitly in all the proposals. PRIA and Chubb's BEIP for small and medium-sized firms provide no payments to the federal government to cover the cost of the claim payments made by the federal government. The same is true for the BCC program during a five-year economic recovery period that can reset. The BCPP expects the government to use a long return period in calculating the price of the coverage it provides, and this return period may well exceed the actual return, causing premiums to be lower than actuarially justified. Chubb's Pandemic Re for large firms appears to be the only program that does not rely on government subsidies, calling for a program "in which both the insurance industry *and the government* are paid an appropriate risk-adjusted price for pandemic cover."[16]

Several important gaps need to be addressed in all these proposals. Whether and how the parametric trigger would address firms subject to partial shutdown order or firms that experience substantial revenue decline but are not subject to a closure order need to be worked through. PRIA might not result in broader coverage for pandemic losses if the underlying BI policies retain a requirement that revenue declines be caused by physical damage. In addition, standard BI coverage can include payroll and benefits for all employees, but provisions vary. If a goal is to maintain employment during a pandemic, PRIA may need to be modified to make it clear that policies would be required to support payroll and benefits for all employees (up to a certain limit), not just those who are difficult to replace if laid off.[17] Insurer participation is voluntary in all proposals except the BCC's. The potential for and consequences of low insurer participation are not addressed.

In following chapters, we model the potential effects of programs motivated by the BCPP, Chubb, and PRIA proposals. The results for these programs give insights into the performance of the Zurich and BCC programs; we do not separately model the Zurich and BCC programs. The ZPPP can perform quite similarly to the BCPP if insurers decide to retain only a very small portion of the risk or perform more like the Chubb program if insurers retain more risk. Zurich projects that 99 percent of risk will be transferred to the government at least initially and, if so, will look similar to the BCPP in the first years of the program.

---

16 Chubb, 2020, p. 4; italics added.

17 The potential for captive insurers to undermine the performance of the PRIA should also be considered. Captive insurers, which can provide coverage to a single insured, have come under much criticism in TRIP. Given that PRIA is modeled on TRIP, similar concerns are relevant for PRIA. For discussion of the captive insurer issue, see Centers for Better Insurance, *Terrorism Risk Insurance Act: Shifting Risk Through Terrorism Insurance Captives*, Frederick, Md., 2020.

The BCC's nondamage parametric BI insurance program has much in common with the BCPP and Chubb proposals, and we do not model it separately for the same reasons that we do not model the ZPPP. The other component of the BCC proposal expands coverage beyond the revenue replacement needed to maintain payroll, benefits, and ongoing operating expenses. Although coverage for various additional costs or liabilities that firms could face during a pandemic are potentially an important part of overall strategy to increase business resilience to pandemic risk, evaluating programs to increase the availability and affordability of such coverage is beyond the scope of this analysis.

CHAPTER THREE

Modeling Approach and Base-Case Parameters

In this chapter, we first discuss our approach to modeling the effects of the proposed pandemic risk insurance programs on relevant outcomes. To do so, we describe the model inputs, the outputs, and the criteria used to evaluate program performance. We then motivate and specify the values for the input parameters used in the base-case simulations. As explained at the end of Chapter Two, we model the BCPP, Chubb, and PRIA proposals. The models are based on a number of simplifying assumptions for each program. In some cases, these assumptions were necessary because the program proposal was silent on a particular issue. In others, we made assumptions to simplify comparisons across programs. For example, the coverages provided by many of the proposals are similar but not identical. We standardized the coverage to allow use of an insurance demand function that enabled us to compare take-up rates across programs. Thus, we project outcomes for insurance programs that are similar, but not identical, to those proposed. Harmonizing some aspects of the proposals allows us to better highlight the strengths and weaknesses of the different approaches.

Modeling Approach

As shown in Table 3.1, the pandemic risk insurance model takes as inputs the features of the risk, program and policy features, take-up rate for the BCPP, and the price elasticity of demand. It then predicts outputs, such as insured loss, the premium, program expenses, and the allocation of cost and risk between the private and public sectors. These outputs can then be used to construct the following performance metrics: the percentage of loss insured, program efficiency, the premium, risk borne by commercial insurers, and the share of program costs covered by premiums. In the remainder of the chapter, we detail the model inputs, model outputs, and performance metrics. The equations that underlie the model are presented in Appendix A.

Model Inputs

The inputs begin with a characterization of the economic loss caused by a pandemic. Our focus is on providing insurance coverage that allows firms to maintain payroll

Figure 3.1
Model Overview

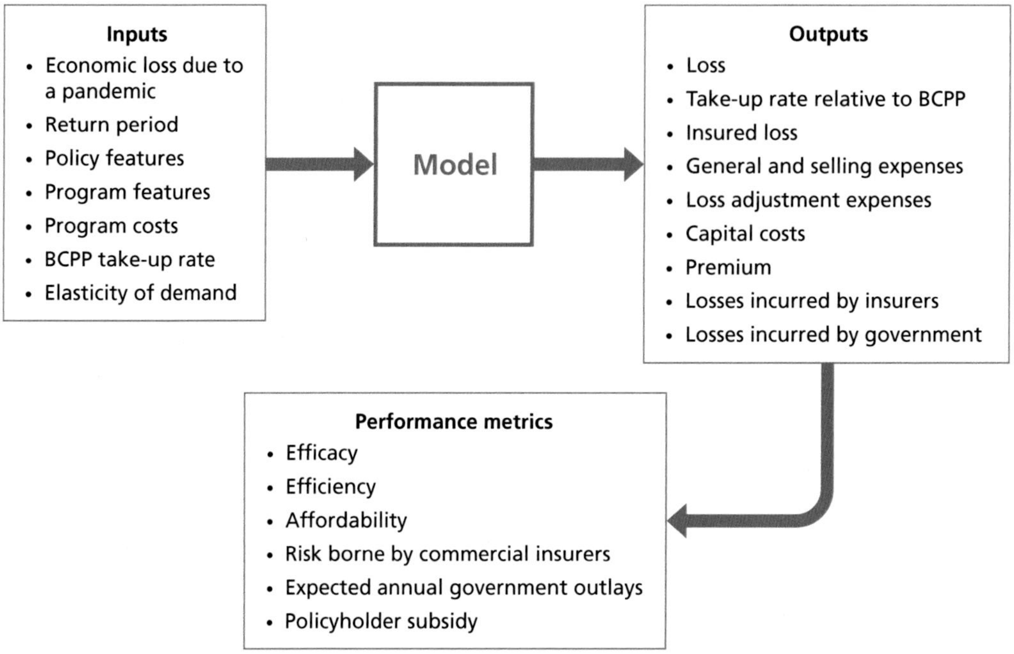

and employee benefits and to cover ongoing operating expenses during the economic disruptions caused by a pandemic. We specify the number of firms affected by the pandemic and the amount of revenue that needs to be replaced in order to sustain payroll, benefits, and ongoing operating expenses at prepandemic levels (see the "Economic Loss from the Pandemic" section of Table 3.1). We model the outcomes of the various proposed programs under different assumptions about the frequency with which a pandemic occurs.[1]

The features of the insurance policy offered to business firms under the proposed program are fed into the model. These include the losses covered by the policy, the policyholder waiting period, the policyholder co-pay for losses following the waiting period, the coverage period, and the policy limit. The policyholder deductible is specified in weeks following the declaration by public authorities that triggers the policy. The coverage limit is specified in terms of the number of months of prepandemic payroll, benefits, and ongoing operating expenses.

Model inputs also include the features of the proposed program (the "Program Features" section of Table 3.1). The firm sizes eligible for the program are specified. For this analysis, small and medium-sized firms (firms with fewer than 500 employees)

---

[1] A pandemic that occurs with annual probability p has a return period of $(1/p)$ years.

Table 3.1
Model Inputs

Input	Description
Economic Loss from the Pandemic	
Firms affected	Number of firms affected by pandemic
Required revenue replacement	Amount of business revenue that needs to be replaced to sustain payroll, benefits, and ongoing operating expenses at prepandemic levels
Return period	The probability of an event occurring is assumed to be a dichotomous random variable with probability *p*. The return period is 1/*p* years.
Insurance Policy Features	
Losses covered	Revenue needed to cover payroll, benefits, and ongoing operating expenses
Policyholder waiting period	A waiting period before coverage begins
Policyholder co-pay	Proportion of loss after waiting period that is not covered by the insurance payment
Coverage duration	The number of months following the waiting period during which losses will be covered
Policy limit	Maximum dollar amount that can be paid to a policyholder in a single event
Program Features	
Firms eligible	Program eligibility based on firm size (as measured by number of employees)
Program cap	Maximum aggregate claim payments allowed under the program
Insurer deductible	The amount of claim payments that must be paid by commercial insurers before government claim payments begin
Insurer co-pay	Proportion of claim payments above insurer deductible that is paid by commercial insurers
Program Costs	
G&SE	Broker commissions and other costs of selling policies and insurer costs of running the program; specified in dollars per policy
LAE ratio	Costs of adjusting and paying claims; specified as a proportion of claim payments
Rate of return on capital	Rate of return required on the capital commercial insurers hold for solvency risk
Diversification factor	The diversification factor captures the extent that insurers can use surplus held for other hazards to reduce the amount of capital they need to support pandemic risk policies
Return periods used in pricing	The pandemic return periods that commercial insurers and the government use when pricing coverage; the return period used by insurers can differ from the return period used by government
Take-Up Rate	
BCPP take-up rate	Proportion of eligible firms that purchase coverage in the BCPP

are distinguished from large firms (firms with 500 or more employees). The insurer deductible and co-pay proposed in the program and the maximum aggregate claim payments allowed under the program (program cap) are specified.

The model requires parameters that are used to calculate the costs of running the program. *G&SE per policy* is specified to capture the broker and other costs associated with placing insurance policies and the administration and operation costs of the program. In standard insurance cost reporting, these costs are represented as a percentage of the premium. As discussed later is this chapter, we take a different approach because the premium does not reflect the full costs of the program in some cases. To calculate costs of adjusting and paying claims, an LAE ratio is applied to insured loss. The ratio depends on the adjustment process—lower for parametric policies and higher for indemnity policies.

To mitigate solvency risk, insurers hold capital, and the rate of return that insurers must pay on this capital is specified. The diversification factor captures the extent to which insurers can use surplus held for other hazards to reduce the amount of capital they need to support pandemic risk policies. The capital cost of a program is determined by multiplying the rate of return on capital by the amount of capital required.

The model does not consider the government's costs of administering and operating the program (however, government claim payments are of course included). As illustrated by TRIP, the government administrative and operating costs are not likely to be large relative to overall program outlays and might not vary a great deal across the programs examined. We also do not cost out the potential government expense of financing these payments. After adjusting for inflation, the cost of federal borrowing is currently very low (and perhaps even negative), and we ignore this cost in our analysis.

To project a premium that would be charged by a program, the pandemic return period used by insurers in setting prices is specified. The return period used by insurers can differ from that used by the government, and both return periods can be different from the actual return period, which is highly uncertain.

The percentage of eligible business firms deciding to purchase the policy (take-up rate) in the BCPP is also specified as an input. The take-up rate in the Chubb and PRIA programs are calculated by the model to be consistent with the difference in premiums across the programs.

Model Outputs

On the basis of these inputs, the model projects outputs relevant to the evaluation of each of the proposed pandemic insurance programs. Table 3.2 lists the model outputs and summarizes how they are calculated. Calculations are done separately for each of the modeled insurance programs using parameter values specified in the next section of this chapter. In the remainder of this section, we provide an overview of how each of the outputs is calculated. The equations used to calculate these outputs are provided in Appendix A.

Table 3.2
Model Outputs

Output	Description
Number of participating firms	Number of firms purchasing coverage; projected separately for small and medium-sized firms (<500 employees) and large firms (≥500 employees)
Loss should an event occur	Shortfall in revenue needed to sustain payroll, benefits, and ongoing operating expenses regardless of whether the decline is insured
Insured loss should an event occur	Aggregate insurance payments based on policyholder waiting period, insurance co-pay, policy limit, and take-up rate
Losses incurred by commercial insurers should an event occur	The loss borne by commercial insurers if an event occurs
Losses incurred by the government should an event occur	The loss borne by the government should an event occur
LAE should an event occur	Cost of adjusting claims should an event occur
Annual G&SE	Annual G&SE of the program; there are annual recurrences of G&SE regardless of whether a loss occurs
Capital held by commercial insurers for solvency risk	Amount of capital held by commercial insurers to hedge against solvency risk
Cost of capital for solvency risk	Amount of capital needed by commercial insurers for solvency risk multiplied by cost of capital
Annual premium	Determined by insured losses should an event occur, distribution of insured losses between government and commercial insurers, return period used in pricing, G&SE, LAE, and capital costs
Take-up rate	Take-up rate consistent with the difference in premiums across programs and the take-up rate assumed for the BCPP

Number of participating firms: The number of participating firms is the number of business firms eligible for the program multiplied by the take-up rate. The number of participating firms is calculated separately for small and medium-sized firms and large firms.

Loss should an event occur: This is the shortfall in revenue needed to sustain payroll, benefits, and ongoing operating expenses caused by the pandemic for all businesses nationwide at prepandemic levels.

Insured loss should an event occur: This is the amount of loss that is reimbursed under the program. It is a function of both policy features (e.g., policyholder waiting period, the policyholder co-pay, the policy limit) and program features (e.g., any cap on overall outlays, take-up rate).

Losses incurred by commercial insurers should an event occur: These are the claim payments that are the financial responsibility of private insurers. Private insurers may be tasked with the administrative responsibility of paying the full claim, but losses incurred by commercial insurers pertain only to that portion of the claim payments for which insurers are financially responsible. The losses incurred by commercial insurers depend on the risk-sharing features of the proposed program.

Losses incurred by the government should an event occur: These are the part of claim payments that are the financial responsibility of the government. The losses incurred by the government depend on the risk-sharing features of the proposed program.

LAE should an event occur: These expenses are the administrative costs of adjusting and paying the claims. They are projected as a proportion of insured losses (using the LAE ratio) and differ depending on whether a traditional indemnity policy or parametric policy is used.

Annual G&SE: These expenses are the brokerage, commission, and other selling costs associated with placing the policies and the insurer costs of operating the program. Annual G&SE should be calculated by multiplying G&SE per policyholder by the number of firms participating in the program. G&SE per firm varies by firm size.

Capital held by commercial insurers for solvency risk: The insurance industry's cost of bearing pandemic risk includes the cost of the capital needed to ensure, with a given probability, that insurers have sufficient resources to finance claim payments.[2] The planning probabilities that insurers are thought to use in making this decision are high—99 percent or higher.[3] The planning probability determines the size of the insured loss that insurers plan for, and the amount of capital that insurers need to hold is the planning loss less the annual premium. For this analysis, we have assumed that whether a pandemic occurs is a dichotomous random variable and that insurers plan for an event that is of the same magnitude as the current event. The planning loss used in our analysis is thus insurer claims plus LAE should an event occur. When insurers cannot spread risk across other insurance lines, the amount of capital required is the planning loss less the annual premium net of G&SE and capital cost. The diversification factor captures the extent that insurers can use surplus held for other types of hazards to reduce the amount of capital they need to support their pandemic risk book of business.

Cost of capital needed by commercial insurers for solvency risk: The cost of capital needed by insurers for solvency risk is the amount of capital multiplied by the cost of capital.

---

[2] The risk that the premium or accumulated capital will not be adequate to cover claims can be referred to as *solvency risk*, *volatility risk* (the volatility of claim payments relative to premium revenue), or *timing risk* (the risk that a large loss will occur before sufficient premium has been collected).

[3] With a planning probability of 99 percent, there is a 1 percent chance that the loss will exceed the planning loss. Lloyd Dixon, Robert J. Lempert, Tom LaTourrette, and Robert T. Reville, *The Federal Role in Terrorism Insurance: Evaluating Alternatives in an Uncertain World*, Santa Monica, Calif.: RAND Corporation, MG-679-CTRMP, 2007, p. 17.

Annual premium: The premium is the sum of expected annual insured loss, expected annual LAE, annual G&SE, and the annual cost of capital required to hedge solvency risk. Expected annual insured loss is the product of the insured losses should an event occur multiplied by the inverse of the return period that is used in setting the premium. We will make different assumptions about the return period used by insurers and the government in setting prices. In some cases, the insured loss relevant to pricing is only the part of overall insured loss that is the responsibility of private insurers. In others, it is the total insured loss.

Take-up rate: The take-up rate in the Chubb and PRIA programs are calculated by the model to be consistent with the difference in premiums across the programs. As described in Appendix C, we use a constant-elasticity demand function to estimate the take-up rates in the Chubb and PRIA programs, given the premium and take-up rate in the BCPP model. The take-up rates for the Chubb and PRIA programs are thus best interpreted as relative to the BCPP take-up rate.

Performance Metrics

Program performance is evaluated across six dimensions: efficacy, efficiency, affordability, risk borne by commercial insurers, expected annual government net outlays, and policyholder subsidy.

Efficacy is measured in the terms of the percentage of losses that are insured (Table 3.3). The percentage of losses that are insured depends on the take-up rate, the characteristics of the policy offered under the program, and the program cap. This measure of efficacy assumes that insurance payments are delivered to the firms that need them and are used to support payroll, benefits, and ongoing operating expenses rather than, for example, profit. As discussed in Chapter Two, further work is needed to flesh out the proposal details that will determine the extent to which this turns out to be the case.

The ratio of claim payments to the overall costs of the program is a measure of program **efficiency**. It measures the fraction of overall resources consumed by the program that result in claim payments to policyholders.

Affordability is characterized by the annual premium per firm, the annual premium per $1,000 payroll, and the premium per $1,100 coverage. Average premium per firm is most relevant to an average-sized firm and does not capture how the premium might vary by firm size. Average premium per $1,000 payroll normalizes the premium by a measure of firm size but assumes that the policy pricing per $1,000 payroll will not vary by firm size. Premium per $1,000 coverage is the ratio of the premium to the amount of coverage provided by the policy.[4]

---

[4] In calculating premium per $1,000 coverage, we deduct the policyholder co-pay from the policy limit. We do not consider the overall program cap in calculating premium per $1,000 coverage, arguing that the individual policyholder does not know whether the cap will be binding when purchasing the coverage.

Table 3.3
Measures Used to Evaluate Program Performance

Performance Metric	Significance
Efficacy	
Percentage of losses that are covered	A higher share of losses that are insured reduces the impact of a pandemic on firms and employees
Percentage of losses that are insured for firms that participate in the program	A higher share of losses that are insured reduces the impact of a pandemic on firms and employees
Efficiency	
Ratio of claim payments to overall program costs	Measures the efficiency of the program in providing insurance payment to policyholders
Affordability	
Annual premium per firm and per $1,000 payroll	High premiums can reduce willingness to purchase policies, increasing the economic consequences of a pandemic for firms and employees
Premium per $1,000 coverage	Premium divided by amount of coverage provided by insurers
Risk Borne by Commercial Insurers	
Insurer incurred loss and LAE should an event occur	A measure of the role commercial insurers play in bearing pandemic risk
Capital required by commercial insurers for solvency risk	When compared with industry surplus, provides a sense of how difficult it will be for the insurance industry to bear the risk envisioned under the proposed program
Percentage of overall program costs borne by insurers	Measures the role that commercial insurers play in funding loss payment and program expenses
Expected Annual Net Government Outlays	
Expected annual government net outlays	Measures the fiscal burden the program places on the government
Policyholder Subsidy	
One minus the ratio of premium to overall program costs	Measures the share of overall program costs subsidized by the government as opposed to being borne by policyholders

Several metrics are used to characterize the **risk borne by commercial insurers**:

- The loss and LAE borne by commercial insurers if an event occurs measure the risk borne by commercial insurers.
- The capital required by commercial insurers for solvency risk reflects the cost of requiring commercial insurers to bear some of the pandemic risk. When compared with overall insurance industry surplus, the capital required provides a

sense of how difficult it would be for the insurance industry to bear the level of risk envisioned under the program.

- The percentage of overall program costs borne by commercial insurers measures the financial responsibility of insurers for claim payments, LAE, and program costs relative to the government.

Expected annual government net outlays are calculated by subtracting annual premium transmitted to the government from expected annual government outlays. This metric measures the direct financial burden the program places on the government. When assessing the effect of a pandemic insurance program on government net outlays, one should compare all government outlays when the pandemic insurance program is in place with government outlays in the absence of a pandemic insurance program. Relevant to this comparison would be not only government outlays for insurance claims but also any assistance the government might provide for uninsured losses. For example, if the government covered all uninsured losses, the government would ultimately cover all losses less the amount of claim payments funded by commercial insurers. Direct government outlays through the program are a useful metric of program performance, but a full analysis of the effect of program outlays would consider the indirect effect of the program on government outlays outside the program. Such an analysis is beyond the scope of this study.

Policyholder subsidy is defined as the ratio of premium to overall program costs subtracted from 1.0 and captures the share of program costs covered by the private sector as opposed to being subsidized by the government. As discussed previously in this chapter, the government's costs of operating its part of the program and costs of financing government claim payments are not included in this measure.

Base-Case Parameter Values

We base the parameter values on the features of the proposed program (Table 2.1) and on relevant economic and insurance industry data. The models are also based on a number simplifying assumptions for each program. In some cases, these assumptions were necessary because the program proposal was silent on the particular issue. In others, we made assumptions to simplify comparisons across programs. For example, the coverages provided by many of the proposals are similar but not identical. We standardized the coverage to allow use of a demand function that enables us to compare take-up rates across programs and to better compare the strengths and weaknesses of different approaches. Thus, we project outcomes for insurance programs that are similar, but not identical, to those proposed. To streamline the following description of the base-case parameter values, we sometimes refer to the BCPP, Chubb, and PRIA approaches simply as BCPP, Chubb, and PRIA, respectively.

Economic Loss Parameters

We start by characterizing the overall size of the U.S. economy. We model the effects of the proposed program on the approximately 6 million firms with employees in the United States (Table 3.4). The U.S. Census Bureau's Survey of U.S. Business reports that payroll for these firms totaled $6.73 trillion in 2017. Small and medium-sized firms (firms with less fewer 500 employees) accounted for 5.98 million of the 6 million firms with employees and about approximately 40 percent of the payroll. Approximately 20,000 firms had 500 or more employees (large firms) and accounted for approximately 60 percent of the payroll ($199 million per firm).[5]

There are also many firms without employees.[6] The U.S. Census shows 26.5 million nonemployee firm establishments in 2018 (a firm can have multiple establishments), with $1.29 trillion in receipts.[7] We do not include these firms in our analysis. Even though the $1.29 trillion in receipts for nonemployee firms is small relative to the $37.4 trillion in receipts for firms with employees, providing revenue replacement assistance for nonemployee firms may be an important part of a pandemic strategy;

Table 3.4
Distribution of Firms in the United States with Employees by Firm Size in 2017

	Firms		Payroll		
Number of Employees	Number of Firms	Percentage of Total	Payroll ($ billions)	Percentage of Total	Average Payroll per Firm
1 to 4	3,698,086	61.7	277	4.1	74,904
5 to 9	1,009,851	16.8	255	3.8	252,512
10 to 19	631,981	10.5	338	5.0	534,826
20 to 99	544,485	9.1	928	13.8	1,704,363
100 to 499	92,358	1.5	914	13.6	9,896,273
500+	20,139	0.3	4,013	59.7	199,265,108
Total	5,996,900	100.0	6,725	100.0	1,121,413

SOURCE: U.S. Census Bureau, 2020.
NOTE: Percentages are rounded.

[5] U.S. Census Bureau, "Number of Firms, Number of Establishments, Employment, Annual Payroll, and Preliminary Receipts by Enterprise Employment Size for the United States, All Industries: 2017," Excel file, March 6, 2020.

[6] Firms without employees are most concentrated in such industries as performing arts and passenger transportation but appear in practically every industry. For more information on nonemployer businesses, see U.S. Small Business Administration, Office of Advocacy, "A Look at Nonemployer Businesses," factsheet, August 2018.

[7] U.S. Census Bureau, 2020.

however, analysis of extending the pandemic insurance programs to such firms was beyond the scope of this study.

Data of the ratio of benefits to payroll are used to scale up payroll totals to include employee benefits. According to the U.S. Bureau of Labor Statistics, benefits in the private sector are 42 percent of wages, increasing the $6.73 trillion in payroll to $9.55 trillion.[8]

Internal Revenue Service Statistics of Income data for corporations provide a basis for estimating ongoing operating expenses. Ongoing operating expenses cannot be easily reduced when firm revenue declines if the firm expects to survive. Examples include rent; mortgage, insurance, and loan payments; and the costs of security services and utilities. These data indicate that ongoing operating expenses account for between 7 and 20 percent of revenue, depending on what expense categories are included in the total.[9] Applying the midpoint of this range to the $37.4 trillion in revenue for firms with employees yields $5.05 trillion in annual ongoing operating expenses (see Table 3.5).

Starting with these estimates of prepandemic economic activity, we use economic data for the COVID-19 pandemic to provide an estimate of the payments needed to maintain payroll and benefits and to cover the ongoing operating expenses needed to stay in business. If the economy completely shuts down, $1.21 trillion per month would be required to enable firms to keep payroll and benefits at prepandemic levels and cover ongoing expenses.[10] However, the economy will not completely shut down. Many businesses will continue to operate, perhaps at reduced levels.

One measure of the economic impact of COVID-19 is the change in employment. Overall employment fell approximately 15 percent between February 2020 (pre–COVID-19) and April–May 2020.[11] The federal PPP, passed as part of the Coronavirus Aid, Relief, and Economic Security Act (CARES Act), moderated employment declines.[12] Some researchers found that the PPP increased U.S. employment by about

---

[8] U.S. Bureau of Labor Statistics, "Employer Costs for Employee Compensation—September 2020," December 17, 2020.

[9] The following expense categories are included for the lower estimate: repairs and maintenance, rent paid, taxes and licenses, and interest paid. The upper estimate adds in the "other deductions" category. Internal Revenue Service, *Statistics of Income—2017: Corporation Income Tax Returns*, Washington, D.C., 2020.

[10] ($9.55 trillion in annual payments and benefits + $5.05 trillion in annual expenses)/12.

[11] Michael Dalton, Elizabeth Weber Handwerker, and Mark A. Loewenstein, "Employment Changes by Employer Size During the COVID-19 Pandemic: A Look at Current Employment Statistics Survey Microdata," *Monthly Labor Review*, U.S. Bureau of Labor Statistics, October 2020. The percentage drops in employment by firm size reported in this article are combined with Survey of U.S. Business data on employment by firm size to generate an estimate of the decline in overall employment (U.S. Census Bureau, 2020).

[12] Pub. L. 116-136, Coronavirus Aid, Relief, and Economic Security Act, March 27, 2020.

Table 3.5
Base-Case Parameter Values for Modeled Programs

Parameter	BCPP Base Program	Chubb BEIP	Chubb Pandemic Re	PRIA
Revenue Replacement Needed to Sustain Prepandemic Payroll, Benefits, and Ongoing Expenses for 12 Months				
Firms affected	6.00M	5.98M	20,000	6.00M
Annual payroll and benefits	$9.55T	$3.82T	$5.73T	$9.55T
Annual ongoing operating expenses	$5.05T	$2.02T	$3.03T	$5.05T
Revenue needed to sustain prepandemic payroll, benefits, and expenses during pandemic	$1.23T	$0.493T	$0.740T	$1.23T
Policy Features				
Losses covered	Payroll, benefits, and ongoing expenses	Payroll, benefits, and ongoing expenses	Payroll, benefits, and ongoing expenses	Payroll, benefits, and ongoing expenses
Waiting period	None	None	None	None
Policyholder co-pay	20%	20%	20%	20%
Coverage duration	12 months	12 months	12 months	12 months
Policy limit	3 months of payroll, benefits, and ongoing expenses	3 months of payroll, benefits, and ongoing expenses	$50M per firm	3 months of payroll, benefits, and ongoing expenses
Program Features				
Firms eligible	6.00M	5.98M	20,000	6.00M
Insurer deductible	$0	$0	$0	$12B
Insurer co-pay	0%	6% up to $250B; 0% above $250B	5% up to $300B; 0% above $300B	5% of losses above insurer deductible
Limit on insured losses (program cap)	None	$750B	$400B	$750B

Table 3.5—Continued

Parameter	BCPP Base Program	Chubb BEIP	Chubb Pandemic Re	PRIA
		Program Cost Assumptions		
G&SE per policy for small and medium size firms	$100	$100	NA	$100
G&SE per policy for large firms	$10,000	NA	$10,000	$10,000
LAE ratio	0.04	0.04	0.15	0.15
Cost of insurer capital	NA	9%	9%	9%
Diversifiability index	NA	0.5	0.5	0.5
Pandemic return period used by insurers	NA	5 years	5 years	5 years
Pandemic return period used by the government	200 years	NA	5 years	NA
		Take-Up Rate		
BCPP take-up rate	65%	NA	NA	NA
Price elasticity of demand	NA	–0.50	–0.50	–0.50

NOTE: NA = not applicable.

2.3 million workers (or 1.4 percent of 2017 employment).[13] Adding this effect to the observed change in employment implies that COVID-19 would have reduced employment by 16.4 percent absent the PPP. Another broad measure of economic activity, U.S. GDP, declined approximately 9 percent between the first quarter of 2020 and the second quarter of 2020 before subsequently rebounding.[14]

Data on changes in firm revenue during the pandemic are not available. For this analysis, we calculate the percentage drop in employment for each month between March 2020 and February 2021 relative to February 2020. The result for each month provides a measure of the proportion of February 2020 payroll that would have to be provided that month to maintain payroll at February 2020 levels. Over the 12-month period between March 2020 and February 2021, these changes in percentages sum to 93 percent of February 2020 employment. Adding 1.4 percent per month for six

[13] David Autor, David Cho, Leland D. Crane, Mita Goldar, Byron Lutz, Joshua Montes, William B. Peterman, David Ratner, Daniel Villar, and Ahu Yildirmaz, "An Evaluation of the Paycheck Protection Program Using Administrative Payroll Microdata," unpublished manuscript, July 22, 2020.

[14] U.S. Bureau of Economic Analysis, "Gross Domestic Product, Third Quarter 2020 (Advance Estimate)," webpage, last modified October 30, 2020.

months to account for the effects of the PPP increases the total to 101.4 percent of monthly employment. Applying this percentage to the estimate of monthly payroll, benefits, and ongoing operating expenses means that required payments come to approximately $1.23 trillion over a 12-month period (see Table 3.5).[15]

Policy Features

The policy offered to firms in each of the modeled programs covers payroll, benefits, and ongoing operating expenses. The program proposals contain different provisions for the policyholder co-pay. For example, the BCPP includes a 20 percent co-pay, while a co-pay is not discussed in the Chubb proposal (see Table 2.1). To facilitate comparison of the different proposals, we assume a 20 percent co-pay for each program. As discussed in Chapter Two, the coverage provided under PRIA would be the same as the underlying BI policy, and a number of issues would need to be addressed before payroll, benefits, and ongoing operating expenses during a shutdown would be guaranteed. We assume that these issues are resolved and that the coverage purchased through PRIA would provide payments needed to maintain payroll, benefits, and ongoing expenses. Unlike standard BI policies, profits would not be covered.

The BCPP and Chubb BEIP for small and medium-sized firms set the policy limit at three times monthly payroll, benefits, and ongoing expenses. Consistent with the proposal, payments are capped at $50 million per firm in the Chubb's Pandemic Re program for large firms. As discussed in Appendix A, there is typically no dollar limit on time-limited BI policies, and we do not include one for the PRIA program.

Program Features

The program features assumed in the simulations mirror those in the program proposals. The BCPP and PRIA are open to all firms, so all 6 million firms with employees are eligible. The number of firms eligible for the two Chubb programs is based on the number of firms in each firm-size category.

The insurer deductible in PRIA is 5 percent of the premium in specified insurance lines. The direct written premium in these lines totaled $239 billion in 2019, resulting in an industry deductible of $12 billion.[16] Under PRIA, insurers are thus responsible for the first $12 billion of insured losses. There is no insurer deductible in the other programs. Above the deductible, insurers are responsible for 5 or 6 percent of insured losses up to a specified threshold (the "Program Features" section of Table 3.5), with the government covering the rest. Some programs cap the amount of insured

---

[15] 1.014*($9.55 trillion + $5.05 trillion)/12 = $1.23 trillion.

[16] National Association of Insurance Commissioners data via S&P Global Intelligence, provided to RAND by the American Property Casualty Insurance Association. The lines of business included in the total are aircraft, allied lines, boiler and machinery, commercial multiple peril (liability and nonliability), excess workers' compensation, fire, inland marine, ocean marine, product liability, and workers' compensation.

losses. PRIA caps insured losses at $750 billion per calendar year, and Pandemic Re caps them at $400 billion. Consistent with TRIP, we assume in the base case that the government will reimburse insurers for LAE on the portion of insured losses that the government assumes.[17] The sensitivity analysis will explore how much the results change when this is not the case.

Program Cost Assumptions

General and Selling Expenses

The insurance industry generally reports G&SE as a ratio of G&SE to the premium. The ratio was 0.176 for the P&C industry overall over the last five years (Table D.1 in Appendix D).[18] Using a G&SE ratio to calculate G&SE in this study presents challenges because we do not have a full premium to which to apply the G&SE ratio. The premium in the different programs is subsidized to varying degrees. What is more, different return periods are used in calculating the premium for the different programs, and these different return periods generate very different premium levels and thus G&SE when the ratio of G&SE to the premium is constant. It seems reasonable to expect, in contrast, that the G&SE should be insensitive to the return period that is used to determine the premium.

A better approach in this case is to estimate the G&SE per policy. Data on G&SE per policy are not generally available, so we piece together information from different sources to come up with plausible estimates. Data available from the National Flood Insurance Program (NFIP) indicate that G&SE average $199 per policy.[19] The vast majority of NFIP policies are written on residential structures. Data on the residential homeowners insurance market in California show G&SE of $222 per policy.[20] These studies both suggest G&SE costs of approximately $200 for residential policies.

---

[17] *Insured loss* in TRIP "includes reasonable loss adjustment expenses, incurred by an insurer in connection with insured losses, that are allocated and identified by claim file in insurer records, including expenses incurred in the investigation, adjustment, and defense of claims, but excluding staff salaries, overhead, and other insurer expenses that would have been incurred notwithstanding the insured loss" (31 CFR 50.4[n]).

[18] As shown in Appendix A, there was not a great deal of dispersion across lines, with the median ratio of 0.21 and 80 percent of the 30 lines falling between 0.166 and 0.370. The G&SE ratio for the line in which BI policies are concentrated (commercial multiple peril, nonliability) is 0.242.

[19] For the National Flood Insurance Program, agency commissions and selling expenses are 28.9 percent of $3.39 billion in premium in 2019. Dividing the product by the 5.10 million National Flood Insurance Program policies results in G&SE of $199 per policy (National Flood Insurance Program, Federal Emergency Management Agency, *The Watermark*, Vol. 11, June 2020).

[20] NAIC reported the G&SE for the homeowners multiple peril line as 26.2 percent of $8.07 billion in premium in 2018, or $2.11 billion (National Association of Insurance Commissioners, *Report on Profitability by Line by State in 2018*, Kansas City, Mo., 2019). Dixon, Tsang, and Fitts reported that there are approximately 9.5 million homeowners policies in California (Lloyd Dixon, Flavia Tsang, and Gary Fitts, *The Impact of Changing Wildfire Risk on California's Residential Insurance Market*, Sacramento: California Natural Resources Agency, August 2018). Dividing $2.11 billion by 9.5 million policies results in $222 per policy.

National Association of Insurance Commissioners (NAIC) data combined with rough estimates of the number of business firms with insurance policies provide a rough estimate of the G&SE per policy for commercial policies. NAIC reports $7.72 billion in G&SE for the commercial multiple peril, nonliability line in 2018, which is the line in which the majority of BI policies are written. Approximately 3.8 million business owner policies (BOPs) were in place in 2018.[21] BOPs provide BI coverage and are reported in the commercial multiple peril line. These two figures produce what is likely an upper estimate on G&SE: approximately $2,030 per policy. If 5 million of the 6 million firms with employees have commercial multiple peril nonliability policies, the average falls to approximately $1,540.

It seems reasonable to expect that the G&SE for the proposed pandemic risk insurance programs will be lower than these estimates for commercial multiple peril nonliability policies. The pandemic coverage will be added on to existing policy coverage, and the incremental cost might not be large. In addition, the streamlined nature of the policy placement process should limit G&SE. We thus set G&SE at $100 per policy for small and medium-sized firms in the base case. It is reasonable to expect G&SE to be higher for large firms. Payroll per firm is approximately 450 times higher at large firms than small and medium-sized firms. To reflect this large difference in firm size, we assume in the base case that the G&SE amount is 100 times larger than small and medium-sized firms—or $10,000 per firm.

We use the same G&SE per policy for all the programs. Chubb's Pandemic Re program and PRIA take a more traditional approach to underwriting and claim adjusting than does the BCPP and Chubb BEIP. However, the pandemic insurance coverage will typically be added to other coverage being provided, and the incremental G&SE in Pandemic Re and PRIA will likely not be as large as the G&SE when writing the coverage from scratch. Absent better information about the incremental G&SE for these programs, we assume that the G&SE amount for the Chubb Pandemic Re and PRIA programs is the same as for BCPP and BEIP.

LAE Ratio

The LAE ratio for the P&C industry as a whole was 0.179 over the last five years (Table D.2 in Appendix D). The LAE ratio for the insurance line in which BI policies are concentrated (commercial multiple peril, nonliability) is 0.11. The proportion of losses from BI loss in that line is likely modest, however, and 0.11 might not be a good estimate for BI policies. BI policies are typically indemnity policies and can require detailed forensic investigation, generating substantial LAE. Data on the LAE for BI indemnity policies are not available, but it stands to reason that the LAE ratio for BI policies is higher than the 0.11 for the commercial multiple peril, nonliability line, as a whole. On the basis of these considerations, we set the LAE ratio at 0.15 for indemnity

---

[21] Figures provided to authors by Verisk's Insurance Services Office via the American Property Casualty Insurance Association.

policies in the base case. It remains possible, however, that insurers will develop more-streamlined LAE for indemnity policies. It also possible that the surge in demand for adjustors in a pandemic that affects the nation as whole pushes the LAE ratio above the base-case value assumed (and results in substantial delays in claim payments). We investigate the consequences of both lower and higher LAE ratios in Chapter Five.

The LAE ratio for the parametric policies envisioned in the BCPP and Chubb BEIP proposals is expected to be much lower. Data on parametric policies that have been used in other settings could provide the basis for estimating the LAE ratio in a parametric pandemic risk insurance program. However, we have not been able to collect such information. What is more, the experience in other settings might not be particularly informative because the number of policyholders involved in other settings is typically small—unlike the potentially millions here. For this analysis, we set the LAE ratio for parametric policies to 0.04, on the basis of the advice of experts we spoke with during this study.[22]

Cost of Capital

In terms of the rate of return that insurers would be required to pay on capital held to mitigate solvency risk, Kielholz found that the cost of capital for insurance companies ranged from approximately 8 to 11 percent above the risk-free rate of return between 1992 and 1998.[23] In a more recent study, Barinov et al. found that the cost of equity capital for P&C insurers ranged from approximately 6 to 10 percent between 2009 and 2014.[24] Because of these findings, we set the cost of capital to 9 percent in the base case.

Diversifiability Index

The diversifiability index captures the extent that insurers can use surplus held for other types of hazards to reduce the amount of capital they need to support pandemic risk policies. The index varies between 0 and 1. A value of 0 means that that pandemic risk has no diversification benefit to insurers and that decisions on how much capital is required to support the coverage are made assuming that coverage for a pandemic is a completely separate line of business. A value of 1 means that insurers believe that no additional capital is needed to support the risk. Lacking better information, we set the

---

[22] Table D.2 in Appendix D identifies a number on P&C insurance lines with LAE ratios in the neighborhood of 0.04.

[23] Walter Kielholz, "The Cost of Capital for Insurance Companies," *Geneva Papers on Risk and Insurance*, Vol. 25, No. 1, January 2000, p. 16. Kielholz's analysis focused on the use and cost of equity. He pointed out that although insurers do use debt financing, it is typically a small portion of the total capital structure (p. 5). This observation, though, applies to the time when this article was written. We base our estimates of the cost of insurer capital on the cost of equity capital.

[24] Alexander Barinov, Jianren Xu, and Steven W. Pottier, "Estimating the Cost of Equity Capital for Insurance Firms with Multiperiod Asset Pricing Models," *Journal of Risk and Insurance*, Vol. 87, No. 1, 2020.

diversification factor at 0.5 and allow it to vary between 0.25 and 0.75 in the sensitivity analysis.

Pandemic Return Period

The pandemic return period plays a critical role in the cost and performance of the proposed programs. The projected premium in each program requires an assumption on the return period that insurers use in pricing the coverage or an assumption on the return period the government uses in setting the premium—or both. In addition, the evaluation of overall program performance requires an estimate of the actual overall return period, which may differ from that used by insurers and the government in pricing. We discuss each in turn.

There is a great deal of uncertainty about the return period for a pandemic the size of COVID-19. Table 3.6 lists major contagious disease outbreaks since 1918 and the number of deaths worldwide associated with each. Also reported are measures of transmissibility and severity used by the Centers for Disease Control to characterize events. The last event of comparable magnitude in the United States was the Spanish flu in 1917 and 1918 (the 1918 pandemic); consequently, COVID-19 is often referred to as a one-in-100-year event. If the 1957 Asian flu is also considered a major pandemic, the average return period based on these three events is 50 years. If the 1968 pandemic, which caused 1 million deaths, is also included, the average return period declines to 33 years. Given increases in population density and global interconnectedness and a changing climate, major pandemics could become more frequent. However, continued advances in vaccine technology and early detection capabilities could work in the opposite direction.

During discussions with informed stakeholders, we heard that insurers will likely assume a very short return period in setting premiums, at least initially. Part of the reason is that COVID-19 and its variants will still be lurking for several years, making resurgence more likely. A short return period may also be necessary if insurance regulators are to approve insurer plans to raise equity capital or take on debt to support the risk. In addition, a short return period may be necessary to convince investors to provide capital at rates that have typically been paid by the industry (see the preceding discussion of the cost of capital). Some of those with whom we conferred thought that return periods might need to be as short as two or three years initially, lengthening if there is no recurrence in the next few years. Chubb uses a 30-year return period in its calculations of likely premiums in its proposed programs, but this longer return period rests on the important assumption that the programs will not apply to SARS-CoV-2 virus or its variants.

We set the return period used by insurers in setting premiums at five years in the base case. The return period used by insurers varies between three and 100 years in the sensitivity analysis. The shorter return periods would be most relevant in the first years after an insurance program is signed into the law, and the law applies to losses

Table 3.6
Major Contagious Disease Incidents Since 1918

Incident	Year	Worldwide Deaths	Measure of Transmissibility[a]	Measure of Severity[a]
1918 pandemic (H1N1)	1918	50M[b]	5	7
Asian flu (H2N2)	1957	1.1M[b]	4	4
1968 pandemic (H3N2)	1968	1.0M[b]	4	3
SARS	2002	775[c]	NA	NA
H5N1	2005	282[d]	NA	NA
2007–2008 flu season	2007–2008	NA	2	3
2009 Pandemic (H1N1)	2009	0.4M[b]	3	2
MERS	2012	858[e]	NA	NA
Ebola	2014	11,325[f]	NA	NA
Zika	2015	51[g]	NA	NA
COVID-19	2020	3.4M[h]	5	4–7

NOTES: Transmissibility is scored on a scale of 1 to 5 and severity is scored on a scale of 1 to 7. NA = not available.

[a] Carrie Reed, Matthew Biggerstaff, Lyn Finelli, Lisa M. Koonin, Denise Beauvais, Amra Uzicanin, Andrew Plummer, Joe Bresee, Stephen C. Redd, and Daniel B. Jernigan, "Novel Framework for Assessing Epidemiologic Effects of Influenza Epidemics and Pandemics," *Emerging Infectious Diseases*, Vol. 19, No. 1, January 2013. Preliminary scores for COVID-19 are from André Ricardo Ribas Freitas, Marcelo Napimoga, and Maria Rita Donalisio, "Assessing the Severity of COVID-19," *Epidemiologia e Serviços de Saúde*, Vol. 29, No. 2, April 2020.

[b] Centers for Disease Control and Prevention, National Center for Immunization and Respiratory Diseases, "2009 H1N1 Pandemic (H1N1pdm09 Virus)," webpage, last reviewed June 11, 2019.

[c] Centers for Disease Control and Prevention, National Center for Immunization and Respiratory Diseases, Division of Viral Diseases, "Frequently Asked Questions About SARS," webpage, last reviewed May 3, 2005.

[d] Centers for Disease Control and Prevention, National Center for Immunization and Respiratory Diseases, "Highly Pathogenic Asian Avian Influenza A(H5N1) Virus," webpage, last reviewed December 12, 2018.

[e] These are deaths since 1982. World Health Organization, "Middle East Respiratory Syndrome Coronavirus (MERS-CoV)," webpage, undated.

[f] Centers for Disease Control and Prevention, National Center for Emerging and Zoonotic Infectious Disease, Division of High-Consequence Pathogens and Pathology, Viral Special Pathogens Branch, "2014–2016 Ebola Outbreak in West Africa," webpage, last reviewed March 8, 2019.

[g] Jaime A. Cardona-Ospina, Valentina Henao-SanMartin, Wilmer F. Acevedo-Mendoza, Katherinn Melissa Nasner-Posso, Dayron F. Martínez-Pulgarín, Abril Restrepo-López, Valentina Valencia-Gallego, Matthew H. Collins, and Alfonso J. Rodriguez-Morales, "Fatal Zika Virus Infection in the Americas: A Systematic Review," *International Journal of Infectious Diseases*, Vol. 88, November 2019.

[h] "The Covid-19 Tracker," STAT, updated May 19, 2021.

due to COVID-19 and its variants. The longer return periods are most relevant to a time after the current pandemic has passed or if the legislation excludes COVID-19 and its variants.

In setting a premium, the federal government might not consider only the best available scientific estimates but would presumably also balance coverage affordability with impact on the government budget. Budget impacts would include both the direct cost of government-funded claim payments net of premium revenue and the indirect reduction in postevent government assistance that would result from lower premiums and higher take-up. Analysis of this trade-off is beyond the scope of study.[25] When setting the premium for the BCPP, we assume that the government in effect uses a 200-year return period. This return period results in a moderate premium in the BCPP—a program in which government bears all the risk. In Chubb's Pandemic Re program, "both the insurance industry *and the government* are paid an appropriate risk-adjusted price for pandemic cover."[26] We take this to mean that government will follow the private sector in setting rates—and thus assume that the government uses a five-year return period in the base case.

Take-Up Rate

Background

Relevant to the projection of take-up rate for the policies offered by the proposed programs are (1) the percentage of businesses with insurance prepandemic and (2) the percentage of firms with BI coverage. The experts with whom we conferred during this study thought that nearly all but the smallest businesses have some type of insurance. Insurance is required for loans and lines of credit, and landlords will typically require renters to carry property and liability coverage. There is more uncertainty about insurance take-up for microfirms (firms with one or two employees), and, given the large number of such firms (see Table 3.4), it is difficult to estimate the take-up rate across all firms.

There is also no systematic information about the percentage of firms with BI insurance. Approximately 3.8 million BOPs were in place in 2018.[27] BOPs are typically purchased by firms with fewer than 100 employees, and according to the Census data, there are about 5.88 million firms with fewer than 100 employees.[28] This suggests a substantial take-up rate BI coverage, but, as discussed in Appendix A, there are

25 See Dixon et al., 2007, for examination of these direct and indirect effects in the context of TRIP.

26 Chubb, 2020, p. 4; italics added.

27 Figures provided to authors by Verisk's Insurance Services Office via the American Property Casualty Insurance Association.

28 U.S. Census Bureau, 2020.

conflicting views about whether firms can and how frequently they do opt out of the BI coverage included in the standard BOP.[29]

Other data suggest that the share of small and medium-sized firms with BI coverage is modest. A survey conducted by Harris Poll Online in 2015 found that only 34 percent of small U.S. businesses carried BI insurance.[30] For the purposes of the poll, small firms were defined as those with fewer than 300 employees. However, Harris did not report the take-up rates by firm size, making the results difficult to interpret. It may also be the case that many businesses, particularly smaller businesses, are not fully informed about what their policies cover and might not report that they have BI coverage when they actually do. Data from another source showed that 37 percent of policies in commercial fire and allied lines included BI coverage in 2018.[31] The size distribution of firms with policies in this category is unknown, and it is possible that these firms could carry other policies as well.

A potential anchoring point for the likely take-up of pandemic insurance policies is the take-up of terrorism risk insurance coverage, coverage that is subsidized by TRIP. TRIP provides an example of what take-up can look like when the premium is subsidized, as it is in the proposed pandemic insurance programs. The insurance broker Marsh reported that 62 percent of its clients had property policies in 2018 that provide terrorism coverage (so called embedded terrorism coverage).[32] Marsh clients are typically larger firms. The Federal Insurance Office reported that 79 percent of policies contained terrorism coverage in 2019 (this figure appears to include multiple peril insurance policies into which terrorism coverage is embedded, as well as stand-alone terrorism insurance policies).[33] Both these studies consider the proportion of insurance policies with terrorism coverage, not the proportion of firms with terrorism coverage.

One would expect the take-up rate for terrorism or pandemic insurance to be driven at least in part by the extent to which the premium is subsidized. More firms will likely buy coverage when the premium is low relative to the losses expected by the firms. We have not investigated the subsidy rate in TRIP, but for completeness and comparison with the projections in Chapter Four, we review the data available on the cost of terrorism coverage for certified events in the United States. In cases when the policy covers both terrorism and other perils ("embedded policies"), the Federal Insurance Office found that insurers provide terrorism coverage at no additional charge in

---

29 Further complicating the situation is the possibility that some small firms may purchase insurance but not a BOP and that some firms without employees could purchase a BOP.

30 Businesswire, "Most Small Business Owners at Risk for a Disaster," August 31, 2015.

31 Figures provided to authors by Verisk's Insurance Services Office via the American Property Casualty Insurance Association.

32 Marsh, *2019 Terrorism Risk Insurance Report*, New York, May 2019, p. 8.

33 Federal Insurance Office, U.S. Department of the Treasury, *Report on the Effectiveness of the Terrorism Risk Insurance Program*, Washington, D.C., June 2020, p. 29.

policies accounting for 30 percent of direct earned premium. When terrorism coverage adds to the cost of the policy, terrorism coverage accounted for 2.5 percent of the direct earned premium in 2019.[34] In terms of the price of coverage relative to the amount offered, the premium was $0.015 per $1,000 coverage for embedded policies and $0.44 per $1,000 coverage for stand-alone policies in 2019.[35]

The developers of the different program proposals have varying expectations for the resulting take-up rate. As reported in Chapter Two, Chubb projects that 90 percent of small and medium-sized firms will participate in its program and 30 percent of large firms. Recall that the program features imply that premiums will be higher for large firms per $1,000 of coverage than for the small firms in the Chubb proposal. Zurich expects take-up to vary by industry and to average 65 percent across the economy as a whole, with premiums at $20 to $30 per $1,000 of coverage. Take-up rates are not projected in either the BCPP or the PRIA proposal.

Base-Case Assumptions

We assume that in the BCPP the government will set premium at a level that results in fairly widespread take-up. Following the experience with TRIP, we assume that the BCPP take-up rate will be 65 percent at the heavily subsidized premium projected for the BCPP.

Price Elasticity of Demand

Previous research does not provide a great deal of direction in setting the elasticity of demand for payroll, benefits, and ongoing operating expense coverage. Michel-Kerjan and coauthors found that the elasticity of demand for terrorism coverage for businesses with over $1 million in total insured value ranged from –0.11 to –0.25.[36] However, their analysis examined the amount of terrorism coverage purchased conditional on the purchase of terrorism coverage. In contrast, the elasticity of concern for our analysis is the relationship between the percentage change in the number of firms that purchase coverage to the percentage change in premiums. Their analysis also excluded smaller firms.

Price elasticities in other settings are potentially also relevant. The price elasticity of demand for crop insurance by farmers has been found to range from –0.30 to –0.90. The insurance purchase decisions of smaller businesses may look more like those of

---

34 Federal Insurance Office, U.S. Department of the Treasury, 2020, pp. 20–21.

35 Federal Insurance Office, U.S. Department of the Treasury, 2020, p. 28.

36 Erwann Michel-Kerjan, Paul Raschky, and Howard Kunreuther, "Corporate Demand for Insurance: New Evidence from the U.S. Terrorism and Property Markets," *Journal of Risk and Insurance*, Vol. 82, No. 3, September 2015, p. 510. An earlier Wharton School study put the price elasticity of demand for the amount of terrorism coverage purchased at –0.65. See Howard Kunreuther and Erwann Michel-Kerjan, *TRIA and Beyond: Terrorism Risk Financing in the U.S.*, Philadelphia: Wharton Risk Management and Decision Process Center, University of Pennsylvania, August 2005, p. 178.

individuals than large businesses, so individual behavior may also be relevant. Estimates of the demand for residential flood insurance vary widely, ranging from –0.62 to –4.48, and one study put the elasticity of demand for residential hurricane insurance at –1.9.[37]

Previous research suggests that the business demand for insurance is inelastic, but the appropriate value when considering pandemic insurance is highly uncertain. Considering the range of estimates for terrorism and crop insurance, we set the elasticity of demand for pandemic risk insurance at –0.50 in the base case. This means that a 1 percent increase in price induces a 0.5 percent drop in the number of firms that purchase pandemic business expense coverage.

Limitations

We examine the U.S. economy as a whole and do not break our analysis down by economic sector or by insurer size. Our high-level overview of program performance is a useful first step and can be viewed as examining average effects across economic sectors and types of insurers. Exploring how effects might vary by economic sector would be a productive area for further analysis.

We have filled in several gaps in the proposed programs. For example, we have assumed that PRIA legislation is written so that the underlying BI policies cover losses from contagious disease during a public health emergency even when there is not physical damage to the insured property. We have also assumed that parametric policies succeed in sending the right amount of compensation to the firms that need it. It remains to be seen whether these issues are resolved in practice.

Projections on take-up rate for the Chubb and PRIA programs should be interpreted as relative to the take-up rate in the BCPP. Given the extent of the subsidy in the BCPP program, expectations of the program proposers, and review of take-up in other settings, we assume that take-up in the BCPP would be 65 percent. The take-up rates for the other programs are then adjusted from the 65 percent baseline based on the relation of their premiums to that predicted for the BCPP. Whether the 65 percent take-up rate for the BCPP is realistic will be better understood as more experience is developed with pandemic risk insurance.

Finally, there is substantial uncertainty about the appropriate values of many of the input parameters. For example, the pandemic return period that insurers use in setting premiums is a fundamental determinant of program outcomes and will depend on a range of factors, including whether the program covers losses due to COVID-19 and its variants. In the next chapter, program performance is projected under a plausible set of base-case parameters, and the analysis provides insights into key factors driving

---

[37] Michel-Kerjan, Raschky, and Kunreuther, 2015, p. 510.

performance. However, it should be kept in mind that the base case predicts performance for only one set of parameter values—presumably for a case that is highly plausible. Attention should be paid to how results may differ as parameter values change. In Chapter Five, we explore the sensitivity of the outcomes to changes in several key parameters.

CHAPTER FOUR

Projected Program Performance in the Base Case

In this chapter, we present results for the modeled versions of the BCPP, Chubb, and PRIA proposals using the base-case set of parameter values. Importantly, insurers use a five-year pandemic return period in the base case. Such an assumption is most appropriate for a pandemic insurance program that applies to COVID-19 and its variants. Projections using different return periods are presented in the following chapter. The modeled programs are motivated by, but not identical to, the proposed programs. To streamline the following presentation, we sometimes refer to the BCPP, Chubb, and PRIA approaches simply as BCPP, Chubb, and PRIA, respectively.

Affordability

Affordability for Small and Medium-Sized Firms

The annual premium projected for small and medium-sized firms in the BCPP approach is $442 (top panel of Table 4.1). This premium is due to the government pricing coverage at levels that ensure widespread take-up, and it assumed that this price is sufficiently low to induce 65 percent take-up. The $442 premium results from what amounts to the government using a one-in-200-year return period in pricing the coverage.

For comparison, the BCPP premium is low relative to the price of workers' compensation coverage but high relative to terrorism coverage backstopped by TRIP. Once normalized by payroll, the projected premium is $0.98 per $1,000 payroll (see Table 4.1). In contrast, workers' compensation coverage averaged $12.10 per $1,000 in the United States in 2018.[1] The Federal Insurance Office puts the cost of terrorism coverage when embedded with other coverage at $0.015 per $1,000 coverage,[2] far lower than the $2.26 reported in Table 4.1.

[1] National Academy of Social Insurance, *Workers' Compensation: Benefits, Coverage, and Costs*, Washington, D.C., November 2020.

[2] Federal Insurance Office, U.S. Department of the Treasury, 2020, p. 28.

Table 4.1
Program Performance at Base-Case Parameter Values

	BCPP Approach			Chubb Approach[a]			PRIA Approach		
Performance Metric	**Small and Medium-Sized Firms**	**Large Firms**	**All Firms**	**Small and Medium-Sized Firms**	**Large Firms**	**All Firms**	**Small and Medium-Sized Firms**	**Large Firms**	**All Firms**
Affordability									
Annual premium per insured firm	$442	$164,000	$986	$1,070	$6.86M	$6,580	$1,630	$696,000	$3,950
Total annual premium	$1.72B[a]	$2.13B[a]	$3.84B	$2.67B[b]	$13.8B[c]	$16.5B	$3.17B	$4.52B	$7.69B[b]
Annual premium per $1,000 payroll	$0.98	$0.80	$0.88	$2.38	$34.00	$2.45	$3.62	$3.45	$3.52
Premium per $1,000 coverage	$2.26	$1.86	$2.02	$5.46	$137	$27.9	$8.32	$7.93	$8.08
Efficacy									
Loss for all firms should an event occur	$492B	$738B	$1.23T	$492B	$738B	$1.23T	$492B	$738B	$1.23T
Insured loss for all insured firms should an event occur	$256B	$384B	$640B	$164B	$59.3B	$ 242B	$128B	$192B	$320B
Insured loss per insured firm should an event occur	$65,800	$29.5M	$164,000	$65,800	$29.5M	$89,500	$65,800	$29.5M	$164,000
Percentage of loss insured for firms with insurance	80%	80%	80%	80%	80%	80%	80%	80%	80%
Take-up rate	65%	65%	65%	42%	10%	42%	32%	32%	32%
Percentage of loss insured	52%	52%	52%	33%	8%	18%	26%	26%	26%

Table 4.1—Continued

Performance Metric	BCPP Approach			Chubb Approach[a]			PRIA Approach		
	Small and Medium-Sized Firms	Large Firms	All Firms	Small and Medium-Sized Firms	Large Firms	All Firms	Small and Medium-Sized Firms	Large Firms	All Firms
Efficiency									
LAE per participating firm should an event occur	$2,630	$1.18M	$6,560	$2,630	$4.43M	$6,190	$9,870	$4.43M	$24,600
Annual G&SE per insured firm	$100	$10,000	$133	$100	$10,000	$108	$100	$10,000	$133
Annual capital cost per insured firm	$0	$0	$0	$148	$64,300	$199	$233	$105,000	$582
Risk borne by commercial insurers									
Insurer-incurred loss and LAE should an event occur									
Per participating firm	$0	$0	$0	$4,110	$1.70M	$5,470	$6,480	$2.91M	$16,200
Total program	$0	$0	$0	$10.3B	$3.41B	$13.7B	$12.6B	$18.9B	$31.5B
Amount of capital held by insurers for solvency risk									
Per participating firm	$0	$0	$0	$1,640	$714,000	$2,220	$2,590	$1.16 M	$6,460
Total program	$0	$0	$0	$4.11B	$1.44B	$5.54B	$5.04B	$7.56B	$12.6B
Insurer share of loss and LAE should an event occur	0%	0%	0%	6.0%	5.0%	5.7%	8.6%	8.6%	8.6%

Table 4.1—Continued

Performance Metric	BCPP Approach			Chubb Approach[a]			PRIA Approach		
	Small and Medium-Sized Firms	Large Firms	All Firms	Small and Medium-Sized Firms	Large Firms	All Firms	Small and Medium-Sized Firms	Large Firms	All Firms
Government outlays and revenue									
Government-incurred loss and LAE should an event occur									
Per participating firm	$68,500	$30.7 M	$171,000	$64,300	$32.3M	$90,200	$69,200	$31.0 M	$172,000
Total program	$266B	$399B	$665B	$1.61B	$64.8B	$226B	$134B	$202B	$336B
Annual government premium revenue									
Per participating firm	$342	$154,000	$853	$0	$6.51M	$5,230	$0	$0	$0
Total program	$1.33B	$2.00B	$3.33B	$0	$13.1B	$13.1B	$0	$0	$0

[a] For the initial year of the Chubb program.

Also relevant in evaluating the magnitude of this premium is the typical price of the property and liability coverage purchased by small and medium-sized businesses. However, systematic statistics on annual premium are not readily available. In the absence of such data, we provide three very rough estimates. First, Insureon reports that the average price of a BOP is approximately $1,200 annually for small businesses.[3] Insureon does not report the size of the firms in its sample, so it is difficult to compare the findings with our projections for firms with fewer than 500 employees. Because BOPs provide both property and liability coverage, Insureon's average price presumably includes both property and liability coverage, but it is unclear whether it includes the price of BI coverage.[4]

Second, NAIC data on direct written premiums for commercial multiperil policies can be used to develop a rough estimate of the price of commercial multiperil policies. As shown in Appendix D, direct written premiums in this line (liability and nonliability portions combined) averaged approximately $41 billion per year between 2015 and 2019. Using the same rough estimates of the number of policies written as in the "General and Selling Expenses" section of Chapter Three (3.8 to 5.0 million) results in a range of $8,200 to $10,800 per policy. Policies in this line are typically held by small and medium-sized firms, but again the distribution of firm size in the commercial multiple peril line is unknown.

Finally, we constructed a rough estimate of the average insurance cost for firms with fewer than 500 employees. Using the Insureon data and input from experts with whom we conferred during the course of this study, we set the average BOP insurance premium (including BI coverage) at $1,200 for firms with fewer than ten employees. We then scaled up the premium for larger firm-size categories using average payroll per firm and then weighted the results by the number of firms in each firm-size category. The average premium across all firms with fewer than 500 employees comes to $4,800 per firm.

Considerable uncertainty remains on the average cost of property and liability insurance for firms with fewer than 500 employees. But if the average property and liability insurance cost for business with fewer than 500 employees falls somewhere between $5,000 and $10,000 per firm, the $442 premium for the BCPP would add between 4.4 and 8.8 percent to the cost of the coverage.

The projected annual premium is considerably higher for small and medium-sized firms in the Chubb and PRIA approaches ($1,070 and $1,630, respectively). These higher premiums are due in important part to the five-year return period that insurers are assumed to use in setting the premium for the portion of the risk that they

---

3 Insureon, "How Much Does a Business Owner's Policy Cost?" webpage, undated-a.

4 When describing business interruption, Insureon says that the cost of *adding* BI coverage is $500 to $1,000 per year. See Insureon, "How Much Does Business Interruption Insurance Cost?" webpage, undated-b.

bear. As will be discussed in the following section, these higher premiums result in much lower take-up rates.

Affordability for Large Firms

The premiums for large firms are comparable to those for small firms in the BCPP and PRIA approaches when normalized by payroll (premium per $1,000 payroll). Due to the market-based rate charged for the risk borne by the government, the premium charged by Chubb's Pandemic Re is projected to be much higher ($6.86 million per firm and $34 per $1,000 payroll) than in the other two approaches.

Efficacy

As shown in the "Efficacy" section of Table 4.1, the assistance needed to maintain payroll, benefits, and ongoing operating expenses during a 12-month pandemic event is constant across modeled programs at $1.23 trillion. Small and medium-sized firms purchasing coverage receive $65,800 on average in all three programs, and large firms receive $29.5 million.

The percentage of firms purchasing coverage (take-up rate) varies across the programs because of difference in premium. The BCPP is the reference approach, with take-up for both small and medium-sized and large firms assumed to reach 65 percent at the premium charged by the program. The higher premium for Chubb's Pandemic Re approach drives its take-up rate down to 42 percent for small and medium-sized firms and 10 percent for large firms. Take-up for both firm size categories is projected to be 32 percent in PRIA under the base-case parameter assumptions. The take-up rates for the PRIA and Chubb approaches should be evaluated relative to the BCPP.

Multiplying the fraction of losses covered given a firm purchases coverage by the take-up rate results in the percentage of the overall $1.23 trillion in event losses covered by the program. At 18 percent, the percentage is lowest for the combined Chubb approach, but it is not high for any of the approaches.

Efficiency

There is considerable LAE variation across the approaches, driven by the different loss adjustment approaches (see the "Efficiency" section of Table 4.1). LAE per participating firm is lowest for the BCPP, which relies exclusively on parametric policies (averaging $6,560 across all participating firms); it is approximately four times higher for PRIA, which relies solely on indemnity policies ($24,600 across all participating firms). LAE for the combined Chubb approach falls in the middle, with the BEIP for small and medium-sized firms using a parametric policy and Pandemic Re using an indemnity approach.

The amount of annual G&SE per participating firm differs by firm size but is not assumed to vary across approaches. This annual G&SE figure is not large relative to LAE when an event occurs, but there are annual recurrences of G&SE, while an LAE incurrence happens only when there is a loss.

The approaches also vary considerably in the annual cost of capital per participating firm. There is no capital cost in the BCPP because insurers bear no risk, and we do not consider any costs to the government in financing the losses it incurs. Capital costs are highest in PRIA ($582 per participating firm), consistent with the relatively high amount of risk borne by the commercial insurers in that approach (discussed further later in this chapter).

A measure of overall approach efficiency is the ratio of expected annual claim payments to total expected annual program costs. Total expected annual program costs consist of annual G&SE, annual capital costs, and expected annual claim payments and LAE. A pandemic return period must be assumed to calculate expected annual claim payments and expected annual program costs. And given the considerable uncertainty about the return period for a major pandemic, we calculate the efficiency for different pandemic return periods. The pandemic return period can differ from the return periods used by insurers and the government in setting premiums, and we refer to it as the *actual return period*. Figures 4.1 and 4.2 show program efficiency for small and medium-sized firms and large firms, respectively. As can be seen, the BCPP is the most efficient of the three approaches because of the reliance on parametric policies and the absence of a capital cost. Program efficiency hovers around 95 percent at low return periods and declines gradually for both firm-size categories as the actual return period increases because G&SE and capital costs are spread over less frequent claim payments. The efficiency of the Chubb and PRIA approaches are lower than that of the BCPP, first because both include a capital cost for the risk borne by the commercial insurers and second because indemnity policies are used for large firms in the Chubb proposal and for all firms in the PRIA proposal.

Although a full assessment of the administrative and loan processing costs of the PPP has not been completed, initial information from the PPP provides a useful reference point for interpreting the efficiency projections in Figures 4.1 and 4.2. The U.S. Small Business Administration paid lenders between 1 and 5 percent in the first PPP draw, depending on the loan amount,[5] and analysis by the *New York Times* suggests that processing fees amount to between 2.6 and 4.0 percent of the loan amount.[6]

---

[5] U.S. Small Business Administration, "Second Updated Paycheck Protection Program Lender Processing Fee Payment and 1502 Reporting Process," Procedural Notice 5000-20091, February 8, 2021.

[6] Cowley estimated that banks fees totaled between $13.7 and $20.9 billion on $525 billion in loans. Stacy Cowley, "Despite Billions in Fees, Banks Predict Meager Profits on P.P.P. Loans," *New York Times*, October 1, 2020.

Figure 4.1
Program Efficiency for Small and Medium-Sized Firms at Base-Case Parameter Values

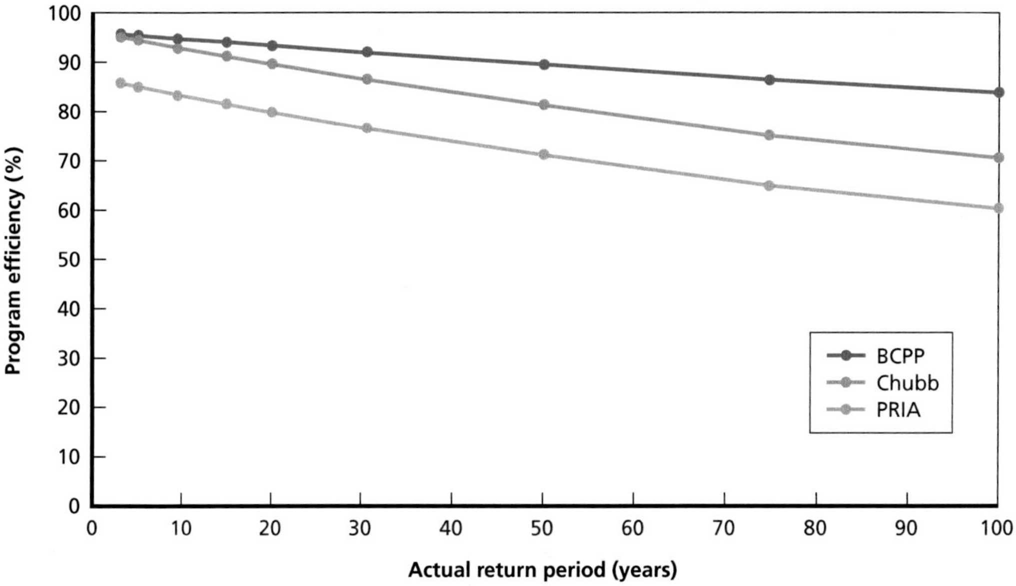

Figure 4.2
Program Efficiency for Large Firms at Base-Case Parameter Values

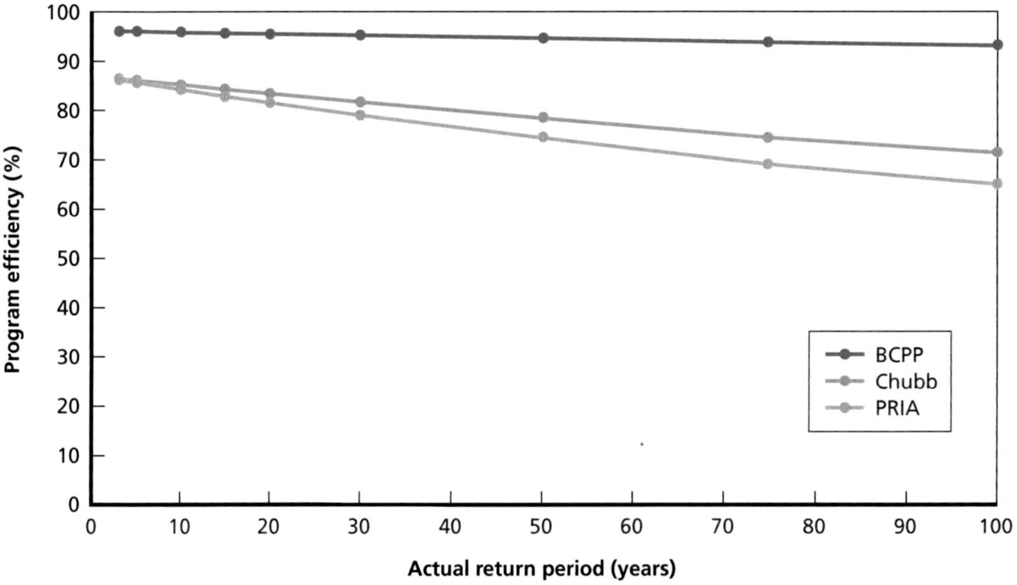

The program efficiency for the BCPP is comparable to PPP administrative costs that have been measured to date for small and medium-sized firms when the return period is shorter than approximately 30 years and for large firms across all return periods examined.

Risk Borne by Commercial Insurers

The programs vary greatly in the amount of risk borne by the commercial insurers, as measured by loss payments plus LAE incurred by commercial insurers should an event occur. No risk is borne by the commercial insurers in the BCPP, compared with $13.7 billion and $31.5 billion in Chubb and PRIA approaches, respectively (the "Risk Borne by Commercial Insurers" section of Table 4.1).[7] The $12 billion industry deductible and large LAE are important contributors to the higher insurer outlays in PRIA. Nevertheless, insurers bear a relatively small share of loss payments and LAE should an event occur, ranging from zero in BCPP to 8.6 percent in PRIA.

The amount of capital that the private sector holds to mitigate solvency risk mirrors the amount of private-sector risk. The cost of this capital is the cost of requiring insurers to bear risk. No capital is required for the BCPP, $5.54 billion is required for the combined Chubb approach, and $12.6 billion is required for the PRIA approach. Recall that the diversifiability index is set to 0.5 in the base case, which means that insurers need to hold half as much capital as would be the case if they treated the pandemic coverage as entirely separate from insurance for other hazards. For comparison, the surplus of the P&C industry was $867 billion at the end of 2019.[8] But this surplus covers both commercial and personal insurance lines and includes surplus reported by Berkshire Hathaway that covers its noninsurance business. The surplus available for commercial lines is on the order of $325 billion once these two factors are considered.[9]

---

7 Insurers participating in the BCPP, as well as in the other proposed programs, may face risk that the government will delay or fail to reimburse insurers for claim payments and expenses. Such risk is not considered in this analysis.

8 American Property Casualty Insurance Association, "Property Casualty Insurance Industry Suffered Largest-Ever Drop in Surplus in the First Quarter of 2020," July 28, 2020.

9 To make this adjustment, the ratio of Berkshire's surplus for its insurance operations to direct written premium is assumed to be equal to that for the other P&C insurers (0.98). Surplus is then allocated to commercial lines based on the ratio of direct written premium for commercial lines to total direct written premium. Calculations are based on data from Verisk's Insurance Services Office via the American Property Casualty Insurance Association.

Expected Annual Government Outlays

The last section of Table 4.1 reports government outlays for claim payments and LAE should an event occur, as well as projected annual government premium revenue. The government receives the premium less G&SE in the BCPP and a large share of the premium in Pandemic Re. The government receives no revenue to offset the risk it bears in the Chubb BEIP and PRIA proposals.

Figure 4.3 shows expected annual government net outlays per participating firm (expected loss and LAE less premium revenue) for small and medium-sized firms. The net outlays per firm turn out to be very similar across all three approaches, even though the approaches have very different pricing and risk-sharing approaches. Net government outlays fall as the actual return period lengthens because expected loss and LAE fall while the premium the government receives (if any) is not affected by the actual return period.

The programs can be costly to the government. For example, if the actual return period is 15 years, the expected annual net government outlays for small and medium-sized firms in the BCPP is approximately $17 billion per year (see Figure 4.4). The lower take-up rates for small and medium-sized firms in the Chubb and PRIA approaches result in the lower expected annual government net outlays for those programs.

The projections of net government outlays for large firms in BCPP and PRIA follow patterns similar to those for small and medium-sized firms. Because Pan-

Figure 4.3
Expected Annual Government Net Outlays per Participating Firm for Small and Medium-Sized Firms at Base-Case Parameter Values

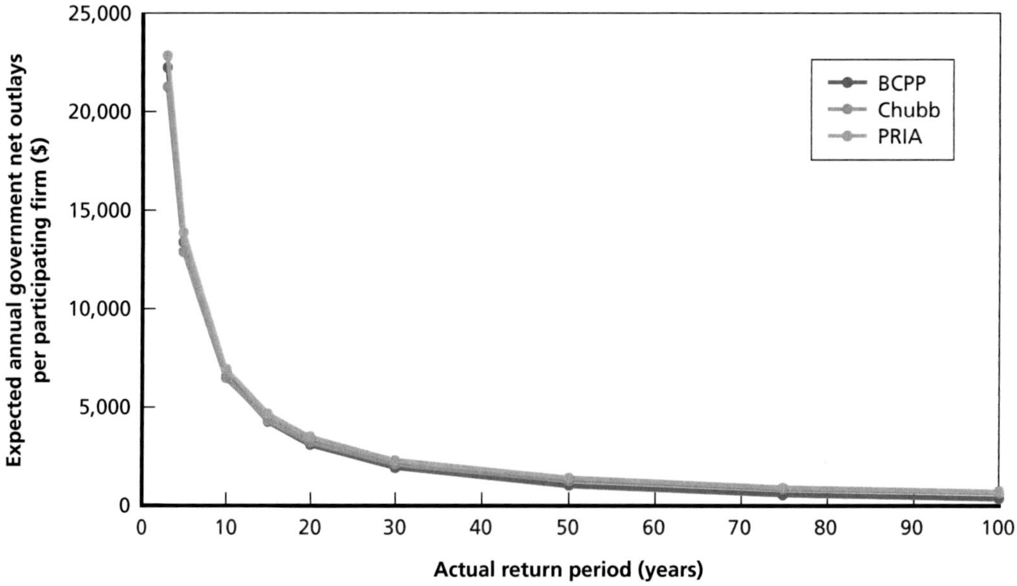

Figure 4.4
Expected Annual Government Net Outlays for Small and Medium-Sized Firms at Base-Case Parameter Values

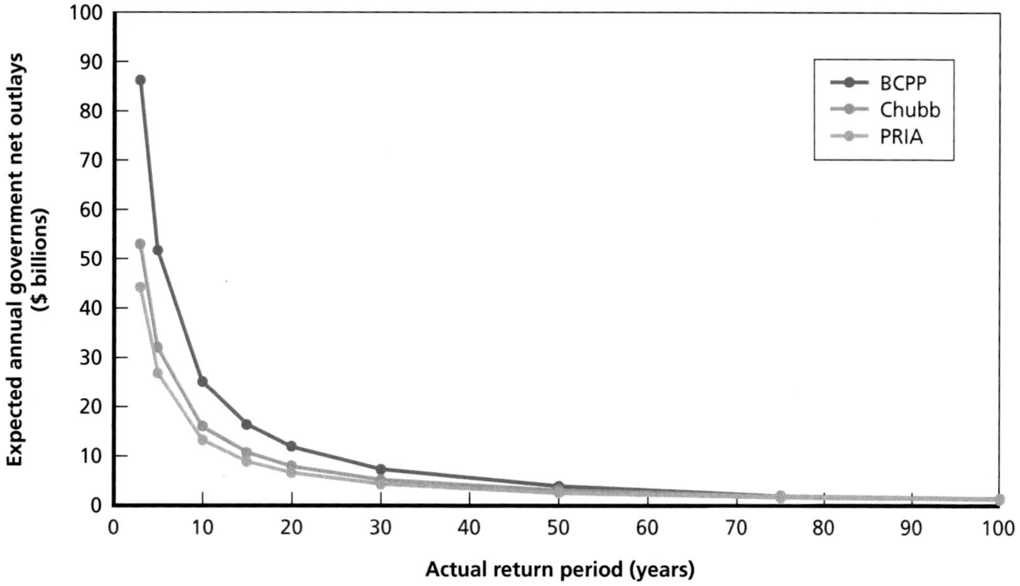

demic Re charges a market-based premium and insurers are assumed to use a five-year return period in the base case, government net outlays will be negative (government runs a surplus) if the actual return period exceeds five years (see Figures 4.5 and 4.6).

Figure 4.7 reports expected net government outlays for both firm-size categories combined. Expected annual net government outlays can be very large when the return period is short. For example, if the actual return period is 15 years, the expected annual net government outlays for the BCPP is approximately $41 billion per year. For comparison, the PPP lent a total of $718 billion through March 21, 2021, with loans averaging $87,000 across the 8,246,234 loans that were made.[10] Care should be taken in comparing the PPP figures with the expected *annual* outlays in Figure 4.7.

Policyholder Subsidy

As shown in Figure 4.8, the premiums for small and medium-sized firms are heavily subsidized in all three programs for shorter actual return periods. Subsidies are highest in the BCPP approach, followed by Chubb and PRIA. For actual return periods of 30 years of less, the subsidies for all approaches are considerable. For example, the subsidy

---

[10] U.S. Small Business Administration, "PPP Data: Find Data and Reports Related to the Paycheck Protection Program (PPP)," webpage, undated.

Figure 4.5
Expected Annual Government Net Outlays per Participating Firm for Large Firms at Base-Case Parameter Values

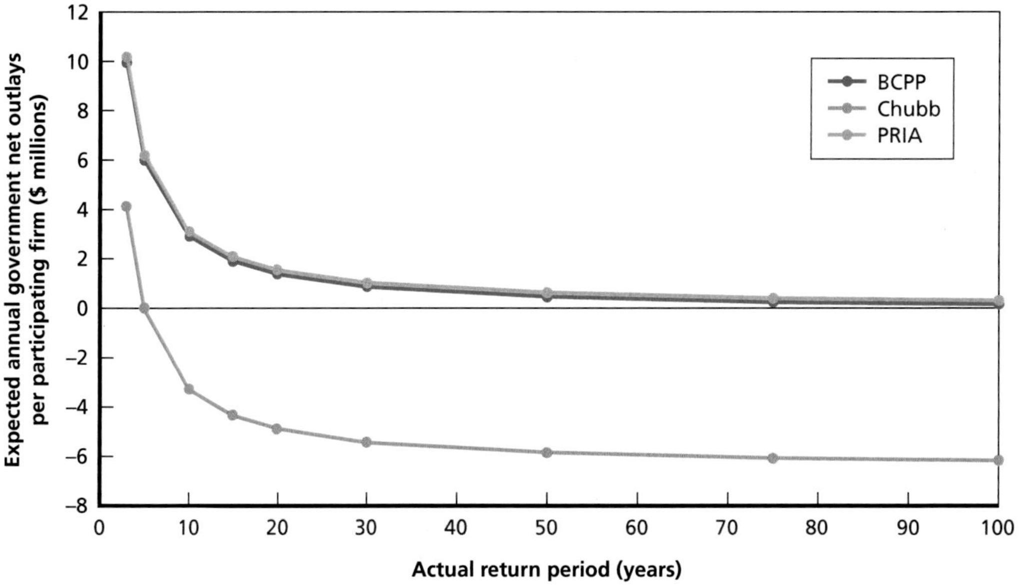

Figure 4.6
Expected Annual Government Net Outlays for Large Firms at Base-Case Parameter Values

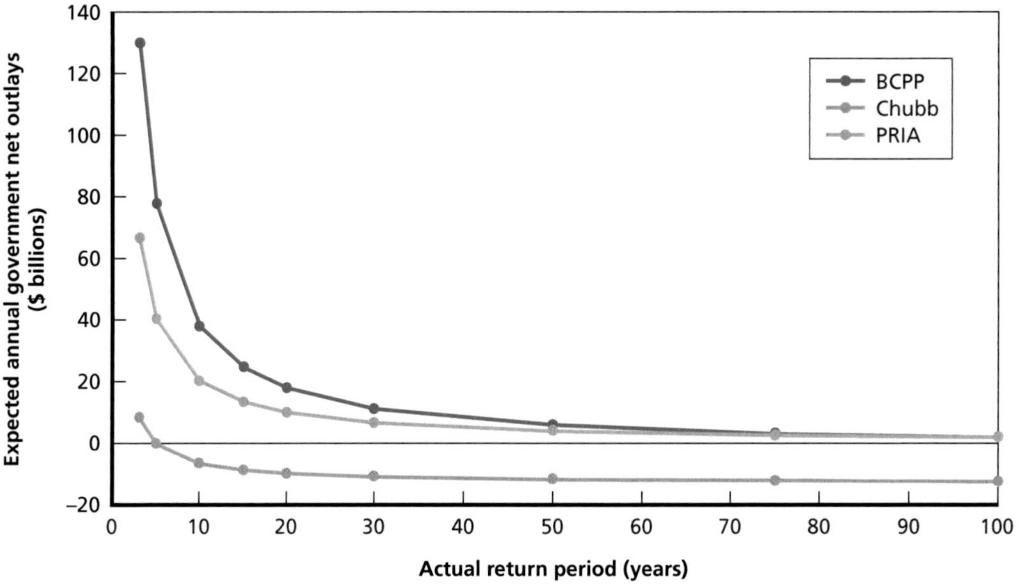

Figure 4.7
Expected Annual Government Net Outlays for All Firms at Base-Case Parameter Values

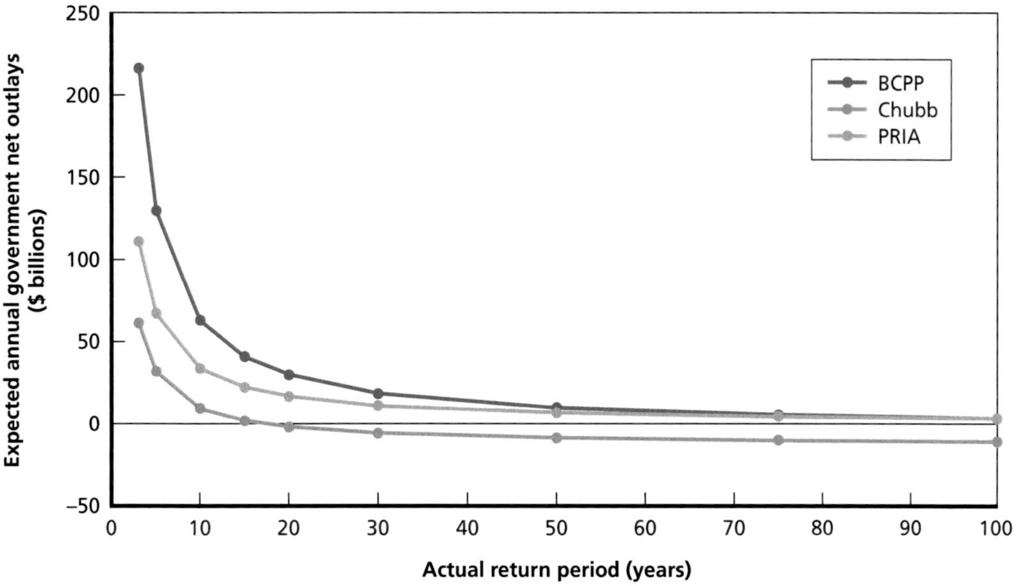

Figure 4.8
Policyholder Subsidy for Small Firms

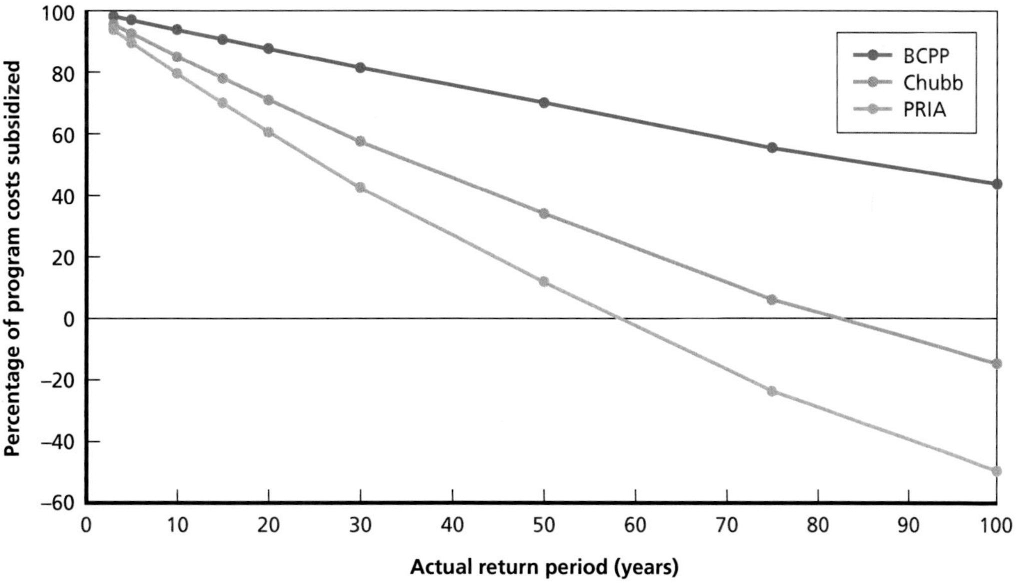

for the BCPP at a 30-year return period is 81 percent, which means that the full cost of the program (for which small and medium-sized firms pay $442) is $2,330.[11] Subsidies decline and ultimately disappear as the actual return period increases. For example, the subsidy in the Chubb approach for small and medium-sized businesses disappears once the return period reaches approximately 85 years.

For large firms, the findings on subsidies are similar to those for small and medium-sized firms for the BCPP and PRIA approaches (see Figure 4.9). Subsidies occur in Chubb's Pandemic Re only if the actual return period turns out to be less than the five years that insurers are assumed to use in the base case when setting premiums.

Discussion

The relative performance of each of the modeled programs under the base-case parameter assumptions is summarized in Table 4.2. For small and medium-sized firms, BCPP performs best in terms of affordability, efficacy, and efficiency. PRIA does the best in terms of expected annual net government outlays and policyholder subsidy. It also does best in terms of risk borne by commercial insurers, assuming that *best* in this context means the most risk borne by commercial insurers. For large firms, the BCPP again performs best in terms of affordability, efficacy, and efficiency. PRIA still trans-

Figure 4.9
Policyholder Subsidy for Large Firms

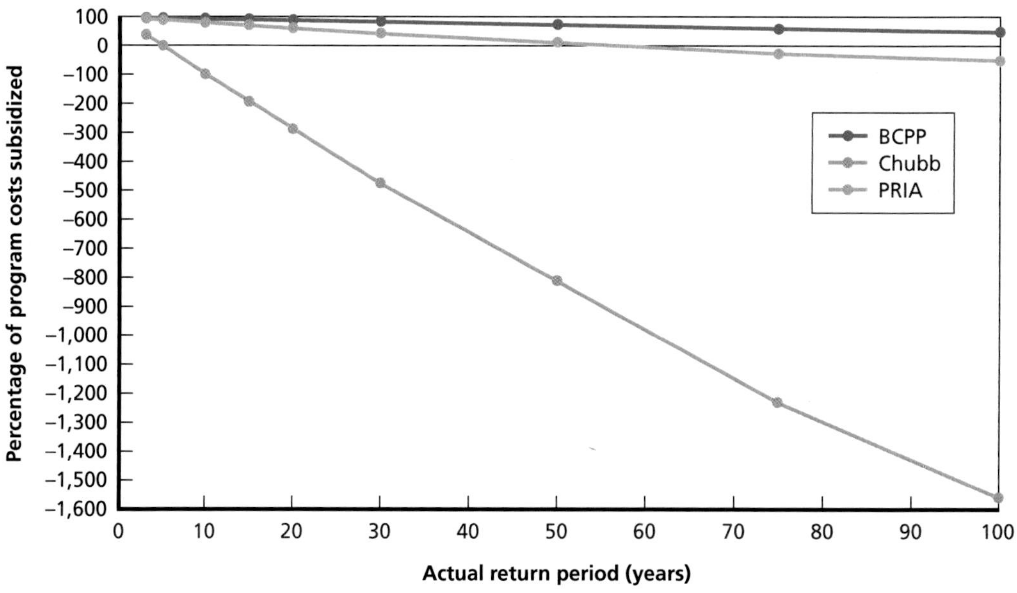

[11] Program costs = premium/(1 – subsidy).

Table 4.2
Ranking of Modeled Programs by Program Metric at Base-Case Parameter Values

	Small and Medium-Sized Firms			Large Firms		
Program Metric	**BCPP Approach**	**Chubb Approach**	**PRIA Approach**	**BCPP Approach**	**Chubb Approach**	**PRIA Approach**
Affordability	Most	Mid	Least	Most	Least	Mid
Efficacy	Highest	Mid	Lowest	Highest	Lowest	Mid
Efficiency	Highest	Mid	Lowest	Highest	Mid	Lowest
Risk borne by commercial insurers	Least	Mid	Most	Least	Mid	Most
Expected annual net government outlays	Highest	Mid	Lowest	Highest	Lowest	Mid
Policyholder subsidy	Most	Mid	Least	Most	Least	Mid

NOTE: Shading indicates the program that performs best on the metric.

fers the most risk to commercial insurers, but the Chubb approach now generates the lowest expected annual government net outlays and policyholder subsidy.

The greater efficiency of the BCPP and the ability of the government to price coverage using a much longer return period than the private sector results in the BCPP's lower premium. Although the $442 premium projected for small and medium-sized firms in the BCPP seems modest, it remains to be seen whether 65 percent of firms would buy coverage at this rate, as assumed in the base case. Very rough calculations suggest that premiums at this level could increase the cost of commercial multiperil policies on the order of 4.4 to 8.8 percent. Some firms may be reluctant to purchase coverage at these rates, remembering the large government-funded PPP.

None of the programs does a particularly good job in terms of the percentage of losses reimbursed over a six-month pandemic (efficacy). This is largely because of the moderate to low take-up rates and the policyholder co-pay. The BCPP does best because its lower premium results in the highest take-up rate. Take-up and the percentage of losses reimbursed for the large firms in Chubb's Pandemic Re proposal are particularly low. Large firms presumably have a better ability to weather revenue declines than smaller firms, but the fact remains that large firms account for 60 percent of payroll at firms with employees, and their financial health will have important consequences for overall employment levels during a pandemic.

Program efficiency as we have defined it is driven by G&SE, LAE, and private-sector capital costs. The BCPP does best on this metric partly because it relies on parametric policies to reduce costs and to address the practical problem of simultaneously adjusting an enormous number of claims. The BCPP also fares best in part because it does not require insurers to hold capital to protect against solvency risk. The cost of such capital is the cost of transferring risk from the public to commercial insurers.

Higher capital costs reduce efficiency but are associated with lower government outlays should an event occur and with other potential benefits that come with greater private-sector skin in the game. These other potential benefits include greater concern about fraudulent claims and the development of the expertise and experience needed to grow the private sector's ability to write pandemic risk. When deciding whether to proceed with a pandemic risk insurance program, program efficiency should be compared with that of other approaches, such as the PPP. We found the efficiency of the BCPP compares favorably with the administrative costs of the PPP, but unless pandemic return periods are short, efficiencies of the other programs do not compare favorably.

As shown in Table 4.2, the amount of risk borne by commercial insurers is highest in PRIA but, reflecting the difficulty of insuring pandemic risk, is not particularly high in any of the programs. Chubb proposes that the insurer risk share double over time—but even so, it will remain modest. One advantage of the insurer deductible in the PRIA approach is that the share of losses borne by insurers would be higher in smaller or better-contained pandemics. The capital required to hedge solvency risk is not large relative to industry surplus for the Chubb and PRIA approaches (3.8 percent of an estimated $325 billion for commercial lines), but further analysis is required to determine how difficult it would be for the industry to raise this amount of capital.

Illustrating the usual trade-off between affordability and government cost, the BCPP approach does best on affordability but worst on expected government annual net outlays and policyholder subsidy. Our measure of government net outlays consists of only the direct revenues and outlays of the program. As discussed in Chapter Two, indirect costs, such as an increased demand for government assistance during an event when there is limited insurance coverage, should also be considered when assessing the full effect of a pandemic insurance program on overall government outlays. Such an analysis is beyond the scope of this study, but the amount of risk borne by commercial insurers is likely a better indicator of overall net government outlays than direct government outlays through the pandemic insurance program.

As apparent from Table 4.2, no approach as currently proposed dominates the others on all the performance metrics. Rather, each has advantages and disadvantages in terms of the performance metrics examined.

CHAPTER FIVE

Sensitivity of Projections to Changes in Parameter Values

There is considerable uncertainty over the appropriate values for many of the parameters that underlie the projections in the base case. In this chapter, we examine the sensitivity of the results to changes in the input parameters.

Approach

We examined the sensitivity of the results by varying the eight input parameters in Table 5.1. Plausible ranges are selected for each parameter based on the information collected during the study.

We assumed in the base case that insurers would use a five-year pandemic return period in pricing the risk that they bear. This short return period would be most relevant if the insurance program applies to COVID-19 and its variants. If the insurance program excludes COVID-19 and its variants, insurers may price coverage assuming a longer return period. Chubb, for example, excludes COVID-19 and its variants from

Table 5.1
Range of Parameter Values Used in Sensitivity Analysis

Parameter	Value Used in Baseline Projections	Plausible Range
Pandemic return period used by insurers in pricing	5 years	[3, 100]
G&SE for small and medium-sized firms	$100	[$50, $200]
G&SE for large firms	$10,000	[$5,000, $20,000]
LAE ratio for parametric policies	0.04	[0.02, 0.06]
LAE ratio for indemnity policies	0.15	[0.010, 0.200]
Demand elasticity	−0.50	[−0.75, −0.25]
Diversifiability index	0.50	[0.25, 0.75]
Rate of return on capital	9%	[6%, 12%]

its proposed program and assumes a 30-year return period in its pricing.[1] Given the key role that the return period plays in determining the premium and uncertainty over whether Congress will require a pandemic insurance program to cover COVID-19 and its variants, we first provide a detailed analysis of the sensitivity of the outcomes to changes in the return period.

For each of the other seven parameters in Table 5.1, we project outcomes by setting the parameter at the minimum and the maximum of the plausible range and holding other parameters at base-case values. The resulting range of projections is then reported for four key outcomes: premium and take-up for small and medium-sized firms, premium and take-up for large firms, amount of capital held by insurers, and expected annual net government outlays. Probabilities are not associated with particular parameter values or the resulting outputs. Rather, this analysis illustrates the sensitivity of the results to the underlying parameters.

Finally, we examine the sensitivity of the results to change in the assumption regarding whether the government will reimburse insurers for LAE on the part of the claim payments it funds. Motivated by TRIP's decision to include LAE in insured loss, we assumed in the base case that the government would cover LAE for its portion of claim payments. The alternative examined in this chapter assumes that insurers will be responsible for all LAE in the Chubb and PRIA approaches. Because insurers bear no risk in the BCPP, we assume that the government continues to reimburse insurers for all LAE in that program.

Sensitivity of Results to Changes in Return Period Used by Insurers in Pricing

The projected annual premium for small and medium-sized firms in the Chubb and PRIA approaches varies considerably as the return period changes (see Figure 5.1). Note that the BCPP premium does not change as the return period varies because no risk is borne by insurers in the BCPP, so the return period that insurers use in pricing is immaterial. The base-case results can be read off Figure 5.1 using the five-year return period. Some stakeholders with whom we conferred thought that insurers might use an even shorter return period if the program applies to COVID-19, and the substantially higher premium that would result from a three-year return period is shown in Figure 5.1 (first dot plotted from the left for each program). For example, small and medium-sized firms would pay $2,760 under PRIA if insurers use a three-year return period versus $1,630 in the base case. If insurers use a 30-year return period, the premiums in all three programs are quite close for small and medium-sized firms.

---

[1] State insurance regulators could potentially resist the use of such longer return periods, fearing that these longer returns could jeopardize insurer solvency.

Figure 5.1
Premium for Small and Medium-Sized Firms as Pandemic Return Period Used by Insurers Varies

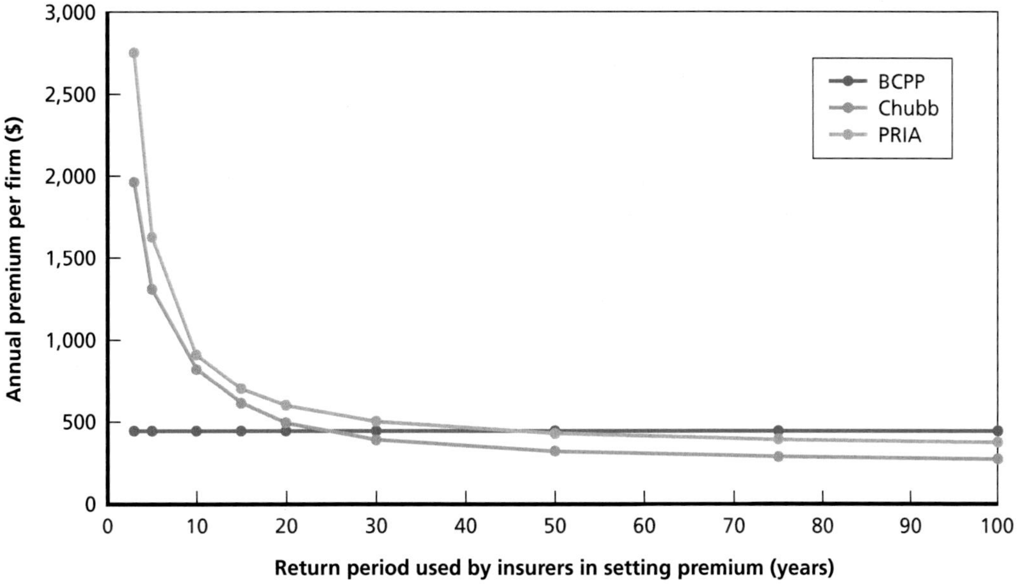

Because Pandemic Re uses a market-based rate for the risk borne by both insurers and the government, the premium for large firms in Pandemic Re remains considerably higher than in the BCPP and PRIA approaches over a wide range of return periods (see Figure 5.2). Even with a return period of 30 years, the premium for large firms is $1.22 million in the Chubb approach versus $164,000 and $190,000 in the BCPP and PRIA approaches, respectively. Only for very long return periods do the premiums of all three programs converge. These results show the challenges of using the Pandemic Re approach for large firms if the program applies to COVID-19 and its variants.

The effect of return period on take-up rates mirrors the patterns in Figures 5.1 and 5.2. In the base case, take-up rates for the Chubb and PRIA approaches are much lower than for the BCPP (see the results for the five-year return period in Figure 5.3). However, once the return period equals 30 years, the take-up rates for small and medium-sized firms are similar in all three approaches. The take-up rate for large firms in the Chubb approach remains substantially below that in the BCPP for all return periods considered.

The amount of capital that insurers hold to protect against solvency risk rises considerably as the return period increases (see Figure 5.4). For both the Chubb and PRIA approaches, the amount of capital approximately doubles as the return period that insurers use in setting premiums rises from five years to 30 years. The amount of capital increases because the annual premium across all participating firms falls as the

Figure 5.2
Premium for Large Firms as Pandemic Return Period Used by Insurers Varies

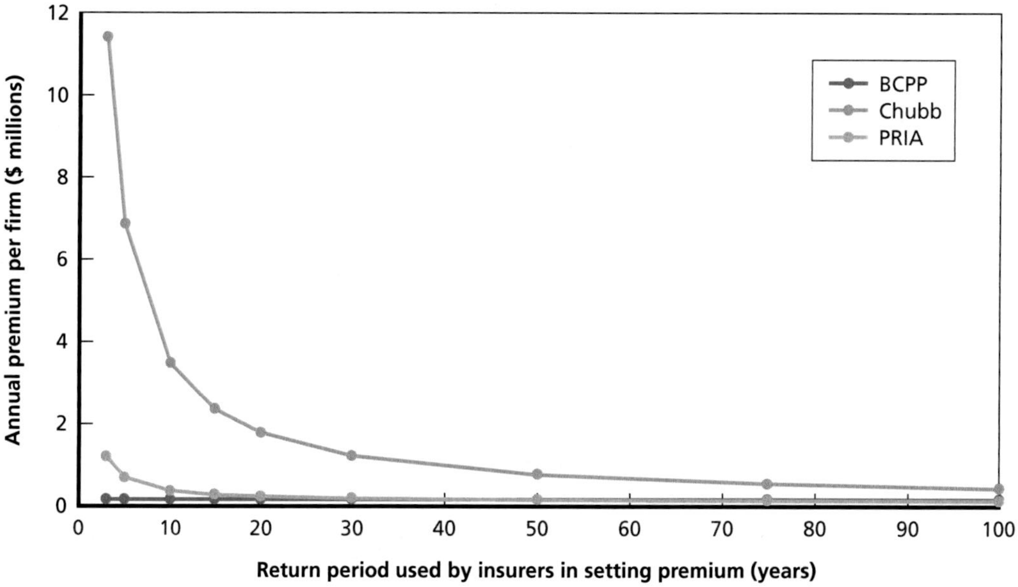

Figure 5.3
Take-Up Rate as Return Period Used by Insurers Varies

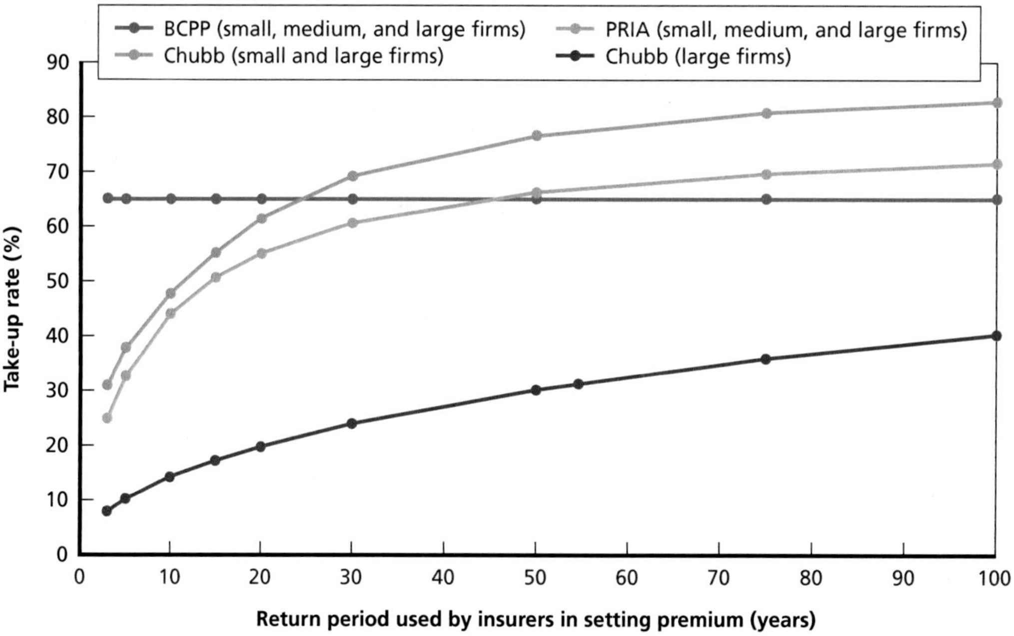

NOTE: The take-up rates for small and medium-sized firms and large firms are the same in the BCPP; the same is true for PRIA.

Figure 5.4
Capital Help by Insurers as Return Period Used by Insurers Varies

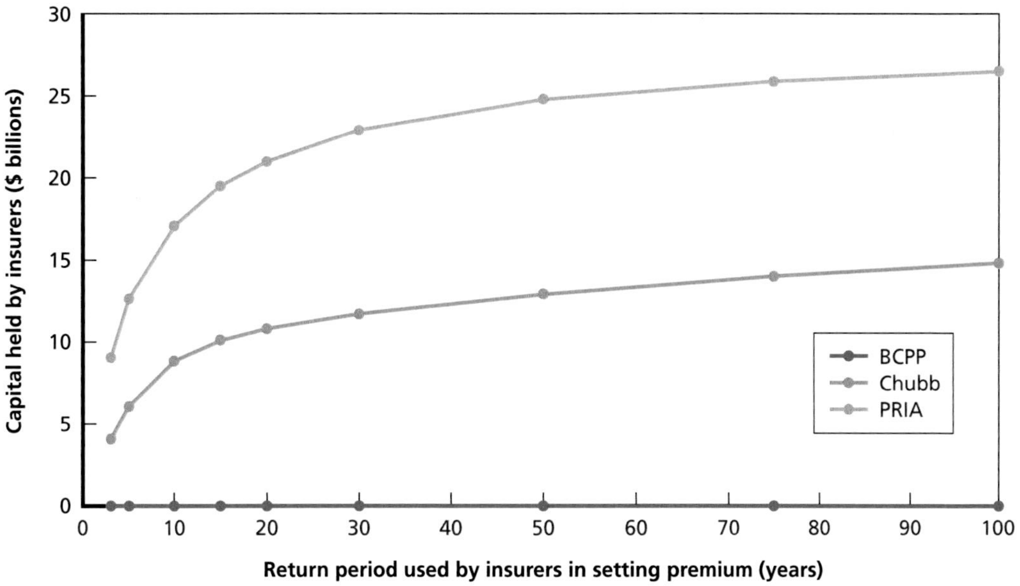

return period increases,[2] increasing the gap between the loss that insurers plan for and the annual premium collected (see Appendix C for a discussion of planning loss).

Finally, expected annual government net outlays in the Chubb and PRIA approaches increase considerably as the return period grows (see Figure 5.5). Expected annual government outlays in Figure 5.5 are calculated assuming an actual return period of 30 years and cover all firm sizes. Expected annual government net outlays in the Chubb approach remain below those for PRIA across the range of return periods examined and approaches those for the BCPP for long return period. When the return period used by insurers in setting premiums is sufficiently below the assumed 30-year actual return period, the Chubb approach generates a government surplus.

Sensitivity of Results to Changes in Other Parameters

Table 5.2 summarizes the sensitivity of the results to variation in the other parameters listed in Table 5.1. The projection when the parameter is set at the left end of the interval examined is reported as the left-hand number in each bracket, and the projection when the parameter is set at the right end of the interval examined is reported as the right-hand number in each bracket. Outcomes that are particularly sensitive to variation of the parameter over the range examined are shaded.

---

2 This result is a consequence of the inelastic demand curve.

Figure 5.5
Expected Annual Government Net Outlays for All Firms as the Return Period Used by Insurers Varies

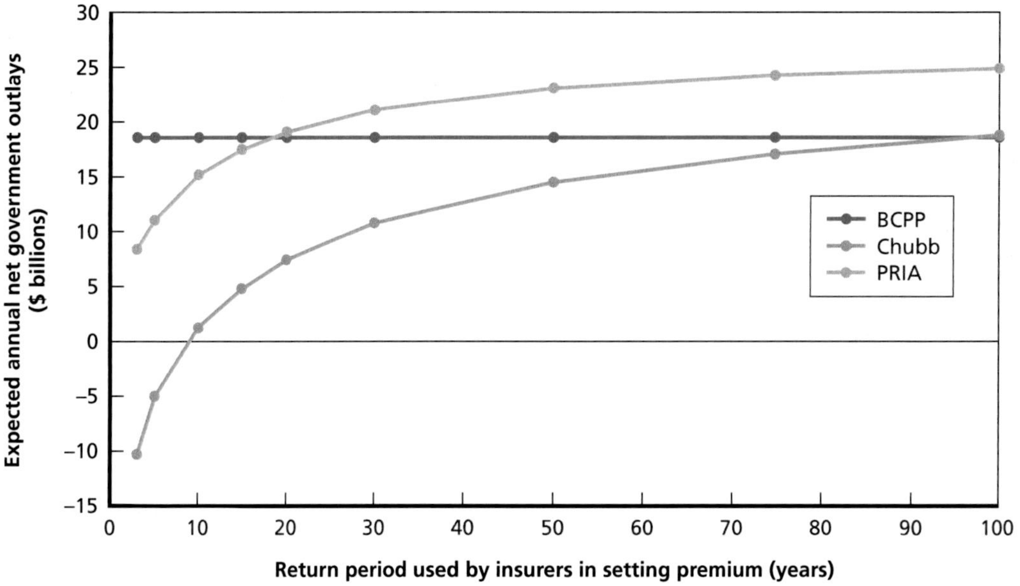

NOTE: Assumes an actual pandemic return period of 30 years.

Overall, the outcomes are not particularly sensitive to variation of each parameter over its plausible range, holding other parameters at their base-case values. For example, varying the LAE ratio for parametric policies between 0.02 and 0.06 does not cause large changes in the outcome of the BCPP and Chubb approaches (PRIA does not use a parametric policy). However, some outcomes are quite sensitive to some of the parameters examined. Because of its low value in the base case, varying the G&SE for small and medium-sized firms between $50 and $200 causes considerable proportionate change to the premium in the BCPP, with consequent large effect on the take-up rate. The demand elasticity also has a considerable impact on the outcomes for the Chubb and PRIA approaches, and the diversifiability index has considerable impact on the amount of capital held by insurers in the Chubb and PRIA approaches.

The results of this sensitivity analysis suggest areas in which further work to narrow uncertainty over likely parameter values would be most useful.

Sensitivity of Results to Change in Assumption on Whether Government Pays Loss Adjustment Expenses

The first set of rows in Table 5.3 reproduces the base-case results in which the government reimburses insurers for the LAE on the portion of the loss it funds. The second

Table 5.2
Sensitivity of Program Outcomes to Changes in Parameter Values

	Small and Medium-Sized Firms		Large Firms		All Firms	
Parameter [parameter range]	Premium ($ per firm)	Take-Up Rate (%)	Premium ($1,000 per firm)	Take-Up Rate (%)	Amount of Capital Held by Insurers ($ billions)	Expected Annual Government Net Outlays ($ billions)[a]
G&SE for small firms and medium-sized firms [$50, $200]						
BCPP	[382, 542]	[69, 59]	[164, 164]	[65, 65]	[0, 0]	[19.1, 17.8]
Chubb	[1,260, 1,410]	[38, 36]	[6,860, 6,860]	[10,10]	[6.16, 5.90]	[–4.84, –5.17]
PRIA	[1,580, 1,740]	[33, 32]	[694, 701]	[33, 32]	[12.7, 12.5]	[11.2, 10.9]
G&SE for large firms [$5,000, $20,000]						
BCPP	[442, 442]	[65, 65]	[159, 173]	[65, 62]	[0, 0]	[18.8, 18.3]
Chubb	[1,311, 1,311]	[38, 38]	[6,860, 6,870]	[10, 10]	[6.06, 6.08]	[–4.96, –4.95]
PRIA	[1,630, 1,630]	[33, 32]	[690, 708]	[33, 32]	[12.6, 12.6]	[11.1, 11.0]
LAE ratio for parametric policies [0.02, 0.06]						
BCPP	[436, 349]	[65, 65]	[161, 166]	[66, 65]	[0, 0]	[18.4, 18.8]
Chubb	[1,290, 1,330]	[38, 37]	[6,860, 6,860]	[10, 10]	[6.02, 6.12]	[–5.02, –4.89]
PRIA	[1,630, 1,630]	[32, 32]	[696, 696]	[32, 32]	[12.6, 12.6]	[11.1, 11.1]
LAE ratio for indemnity policies [0.10, 0.20]						
BCPP	[442, 442]	[65, 65]	[164, 164]	[65, 65]	[0, 0]	[18.6, 18.6]
Chubb	[1,311, 1,311]	[38, 38]	[6,570, 7,160]	[10, 10]	[6.04, 6.10]	[–4.71, –5.19]
PRIA	[1,524, 1,710]	[33, 32]	[659, 734]	[33, 32]	[12.2, 13.0]	[10.9, 11.3]
Demand elasticity [–0.25, –0.75]						
BCPP	[442, 442]	[65, 65]	[164, 164]	[65, 65]	[0, 0]	[18.6, 18.6]
Chubb	[1,311, 1,311]	[50, 29]	[6,860, 6,860]	[25, 4]	[9.73, 4.09]	[–20.0, –0.260]
PRIA	[1,428, 2,080]	[48, 19]	[606, 898]	[48, 19]	[16.0, 9.56]	[16.4, 6.33]

Table 5.2—Continued

Parameter [parameter range]	Small and Medium-Sized Firms: Premium ($ per firm)	Small and Medium-Sized Firms: Take-Up Rate (%)	Large Firms: Premium ($1,000 per firm)	Large Firms: Take-Up Rate (%)	All Firms: Amount of Capital Held by Insurers ($ billions)	All Firms: Expected Annual Government Net Outlays ($ billions)[a]
Diversifiability index [0.25, 0.75]						
BCPP	[442, 442]	[65, 65]	[164, 164]	[65, 65]	[0, 0]	[18.6, 18.6]
Chubb	[1,400, 1,220]	[36, 39]	[6,900, 6,830]	[10, 10]	[8.91, 3.11]	[–5.19, –4.70]
PRIA	[1,780, 1,490]	[31, 34]	[763, 632]	[31, 34]	[18.4, 6.48]	[10.6, 11.7]
Rate of return on capital [0.06, 0.12]						
BCPP	[442, 442]	[65, 65]	[164, 164]	[65, 65]	[0, 0]	[18.6, 18.6]
Chubb	[1,250, 1,370]	[39, 37]	[6,840, 6,890]	[10, 10]	[6.16, 5.98]	[–4.79, –5.12]
PRIA	[1,530, 1,730]	[34, 32]	[653, 740]	[34, 32]	[12.8, 12.4]	[11.5, 10.8]

NOTES: Outcomes particularly sensitive to variation of the specified parameter over its plausible range are shaded.

[a] Assumes actual pandemic return period of 30 years.

set of rows presents the results when insurers are responsible for all LAE, regardless of what part of overall claim payments are funded by the government. Because insurers bear no risk in the BCPP, we assume that the government continues to reimburse insurers for all LAE in that program.

Requiring insurers to bear all LAE has a substantial impact on premium and take-up for small and medium-sized firms. For example, premium in the Chubb approach for small and medium-sized firms rises from $1,070 to $1,650, and the take-up rate falls from 42 percent to 34 percent. The effect on large firms is also considerable in PRIA, although the effect is minimal in Chubb's Pandemic Re approach because the premium is already at a market-based rate. Capital held by insurers to protect against solvency risk roughly doubles if the insurers bear all LAE. In contrast, government net annual outlays fall as more of the overall program costs are passed to the private sector.

Table 5.3
Sensitivity of Program Outcomes to Change in Assumption on Whether Government Pays Loss Adjustment Expenses

	Small and Medium-Sized Firms		Large Firms		All Firms	
Assumption	Premium ($ per firm)	Take-Up Rate (%)	Premium ($ per firm)	Take-Up Rate (%)	Amount of Capital Held by Insurers ($ billions)	Expected Annual Government Net Outlays ($ billions)[a]
Government pays LAE on its portion of claim payments						
BCPP	$442	65%	$164,000	65%	$0	$18.7
Chubb	$1,070	42%	$6.86M	10%	$5.54	–$5.59
PRIA	$1,630	32%	$696,000	32%	$12.6	$11.1
Government does not pay LAE on its portion of claim payments						
BCPP	—	—	—	—	—	—
Chubb	$1,650	34%	$7.06M	10%	$11.1	–7.33
PRIA	$2,330	20%	$1.01M	20%	$20.6	$5.90

[a] Assumes actual pandemic return period of 30 years.

CHAPTER SIX

Conclusion

Several programs have been proposed to expand the availability of insurance for business revenue declines due to pandemic-induced business closures or restrictions on business activity. These programs seek to keep employee paychecks coming during a pandemic and to cover the ongoing operating expenses needed for firms to survive until the pandemic passes. The programs differ in several key dimensions, including the amount of risk borne by commercial insurers, the approach to paying claims, the extent to which the U.S. government receives a premium for the risk it bears, and the extent of policyholder subsidies.

The programs all leverage the deep capability of the commercial insurance industry to place policies and adjust claims. The programs all seek to define benefits and the benefit distribution mechanism in advance rather than rely on programs hastily crafted after an event occurs.

The programs were modeled and performance characterized in the following dimensions:

- efficacy
- efficiency
- affordability
- risk borne by commercial insurers
- expected annual government outlays
- extent of policyholder subsidy.

For small and medium-sized firms, the BCPP approach performs best in terms of affordability, efficacy, and efficiency. The PRIA approach does the best in terms of expected annual net government outlays and policyholder subsidy. It also does best in terms of risk borne by commercial insurers, assuming that *best* in this context means the most risk borne by commercial insurers. For large firms, the BCPP again performs best in terms of affordability, efficacy, and efficiency. PRIA still transfers the most risk to commercial insurers, but the Chubb approach now generates the lowest expected annual government net outlays and policyholder subsidy. Projected outcomes are sensitive to a number of underlying model parameters, about which there is considerable uncertainly. In particular, the pandemic return period that insurers used in pricing coverage has an important impact on premium and take-up in the Chubb and PRIA approaches, with the return period used in pricing depending importantly on whether the program applies to COVID-19 and its variants.

This analysis provides information useful to assessing the advantages and disadvantages of different approaches for improving the availability and affordability of pandemic risk insurance. However, it does not seek to evaluate and compare the full range of policy options for addressing pandemic losses. Such a policy analysis would systematically compare the advantages and disadvantages of an insurance-based approach with a government-based approach, such as the PPP. It would also take a more comprehensive view of some of the outcome measures used in this analysis. For example, in this report we have projected government net outlays directly through the proposed programs, but a more comprehensive analysis would include the indirect effects of the program on other government outlays.

The various proposals that we have examined contain several important gaps that remain to be filled—for example,

- whether and how the parametric trigger would address firms either subject to a partial shutdown order or that experience substantial revenue decline but are not subject to a closure order
- whether policies backed by PRIA will provide coverage for pandemic losses when the underlying BI policies require physical damage to the insured property
- whether parametric policies will result in some firms receiving more compensation than they need and others less (basis risk).

In this analysis, we have in effect assumed that gaps are filled in that result in the right amount of assistance getting to the right firms, but additional work is needed to flesh out the proposals to deal with these and other gaps and to determine the extent to which unaddressed issues can be resolved.

APPENDIX A

Overview of Business Interruption Policies

BI insurance, also known as *business income and extra expense insurance*, covers net income that would have been earned during the period of interruption plus continuing normal operating expenses.[1] The provisions of the BI policies can vary, and the following overview attempts to characterize the policies typically held by small and medium-sized businesses.[2]

BI coverage is typically tied to a property policy. It is included in the standard BOP and is primarily designed to cover loss of business income due to suspension of operations caused by direct physical damage to the covered property. The physical damage must be caused by a hazard covered by the policy (a *covered cause of loss*).[3] The policy covers net income (profit) that would have been earned or incurred if no physical loss or damage had occurred, as well as *continuing normal operating expenses*. Coverage applies during the period required to repair the damaged property or to find a new location, up to 12 consecutive months.

Continuing normal operating expenses include such items as rent, loan payments, utilities, and payroll.[4] However, the standard policy does not treat the payroll of all employees the same. Payroll for officers, executives, managers, employees under contract, and other specified job classes are covered for up to 12 consecutive months. These are generally employees with hard-to-replace skills. Payroll for everyone else is referred to as *ordinary payroll*, and ordinary payroll is covered for 60 days in the standard policy. There was disagreement among the experts with whom we conferred during the course of this study about how frequently firms that purchase property insurance have BI coverage. Some maintained that there are limited options to opt out

1 Elsewhere in the report we use the term *business revenue* rather than *business income* and do not distinguish between the two terms.

2 This overview is based in part on Insurance Services Office, Businessowners Coverage Form, BP 00 03 01 10, 2009.

3 Insurance Services Office, 2009.

4 In this report, *ongoing operating expenses* refers to that part of normal operating expenses other than payroll and benefits.

of the BI coverage included in the standard BOP. Others said that small businesses in the United States typically opt out of ordinary payroll coverage.

Continuing normal operating expenses are not explicitly defined in the standard policy, which is one of the reasons that business income losses are more costly to adjust than losses in many other lines of insurance.

There is typically no dollar limit on this time-based coverage. All losses (other than ordinary payroll) in the 12-month period following the physical damage are covered even if the 12-month period extends beyond the end of the policy period. What is more, the 12-month period resets for each loss. Thus, a firm with a nine-month closure due to property damage at the beginning of the policy period and a 12-month closure due to property damage on the last day of the policy period could receive payment for income losses over 21 months. There is also no waiting period before coverage applies (except for the civil authority coverage).

Loss of business income due to actions of a civil authority is also covered in the standard BOP, but not nearly to the same extent as losses due to the suspension of operations caused by physical damage to the insured property. Coverage applies when the insured property is in the area closed because of the incident and no more than one mile from the damaged property. Coverage typically begins 72 hours after the closure and applies for four consecutive weeks following the closure.

APPENDIX B

Insurance Payments in a Partial Shutdown

This appendix shows how much of a parametric payout a firm would need to return (or reserve for future use) during a partial shutdown. The analysis assumes that firms are not reimbursed for lost profits and are provided with enough income to maintain payroll and benefits at preshutdown levels and to cover ongoing operating expenses postshutdown.

Monthly firm revenue preshutdown is the sum of the following components:

$$I_0 = \pi_0 + PBOE_0 + VC_0,$$

where

I_0 = monthly income preshutdown

π_0 = monthly firm profit preshutdown

$PBOE_0$ = monthly payroll, benefits, and ongoing operating expenses preshutdown

VC_0 = monthly firm variable costs preshutdown.

When a shutdown occurs, the firm receives a parametric insurance payment equal to preshutdown payroll, benefits, and ongoing operating expenses. The firm monthly income postshutdown is thus

$$I_{1R} = I_1 + PBOE_0,$$

where

I_{1R} = postshutdown income received, including insurance payout

I_1 = income postshutdown without insurance payment and $0 \leq I_1 < I_0$.

To maintain payroll, benefits, and ongoing operating expenses postshutdown, the firm needs the following income:

$$I_{1N} = PBOE_0 + VC_1,$$

where

I_{1N} = monthly income needed to maintain preshutdown payroll and benefits and to support postshutdown ongoing expenses

VC_1 = monthly variable costs required to support postshutdown level of production.

The firm makes zero profit in this situation.

Subtracting the amount of income needed from the amount of income received postshutdown results in the amount of the insurance payment that is returned or reserved for future use:

$$\text{Amount of the insurance payment returned} = \begin{cases} 0 \text{ when } VC_1 > I_1 \\ I_1 - VC_1 \text{ when } I_1 - PBOE_0 < VC_{1C} < I_1 \\ PBOE_0 \text{ when } VC_1 < I_1 - PBOE_0. \end{cases}$$

APPENDIX C

Pandemic Risk Insurance Model

In this appendix, we provide the equations used to calculate the model outputs listed in Table 3.2. Table C.1 defines the parameters used in the equations.

Table C.1
Parameter Definitions

Parameter	Definition
event_loss	Reduction in payroll, benefits, and revenue needed to cover ongoing costs due to the pandemic
eligible_firms	Number of firms eligible to participate in program
covered_costs_per_month	Payroll, benefits, and ongoing operating expenses covered by the policy in dollars per month
dindex	The diversifiability index factor, which captures the extent that insurers can use surplus held for other types of hazards to reduce the amount of capital they need to support pandemic risk policies
months_coverage	Months of costs provided by policy
pholder_deductible	The amount of loss absorbed by the policyholder before insurance payments begin
pholder_copay	Proportion of loss after waiting period that is not covered by the insurance payment
program_cap	Maximum aggregate claim payments allowed under the program
insurer_deductible	The amount of claim payments that must be paid by commercial insurers before government claim payments begin
insurer_copay	Proportion of claim payments above insurer deductible that is paid by commercial insurers
ror	Rate of return required on the capital that commercial insurers hold for solvency risk
event_prob	The pandemic return periods that commercial insurers or the government use in pricing coverage; the return period used by insurers can differ from that used by government
lae_ratio	Ratio applied to claim payments to calculate LAE
takeup	Proportion of eligible firms that purchase coverage

The number of firms participating in the program is

$$participating\_firms = eligible\_firms * takeup. \tag{C.1}$$

The number is calculated separately for small and medium-sized and large firms.

The maximum amount of loss covered by the policy is

$$policy\_limit = covered\_costs\_per\_month * months\_coverage. \tag{C.2}$$

Losses that occur any time during the policy period are covered up to the policy limit. The policy limit for Pandemic Re is the $50 million dollar limit prescribed in the Chubb's proposal multiplied by the number of participating firms.

The amount of loss that is insured should an event occur is

$$\begin{aligned} &insured\_loss = \\ &\min(takeup * (event\_loss - pholder\_deductible) * (1 - pholder\_copay), \\ &takeup * (policy\_limit - pholder\_deductible) * (1 - pholder\_copay), \\ &program\_cap). \end{aligned} \tag{C.3}$$

The amount of insured loss incurred by insurers should an event occur is

$$insurer\_claims = \begin{cases} insured\_loss \text{ if } insured\_loss \leq insurer\_deductible \\ insurer\_deductible + insurer\_copay * (insured\_loss - insurer\_deductible) \\ if\ insured\_loss > insurer\_deductible. \end{cases} \tag{C.4}$$

$$govt\_claims = insured\_loss - insurer\_claims. \tag{C.5}$$

$$LAE = insured\_loss * LAE\_ratio. \tag{C.6}$$

$$G\&SE = \begin{cases} \$100 \text{ for small and medium-sized firms} \\ \$10{,}000 \text{ for large firms} \end{cases}. \tag{C.7}$$

The insurance industry's cost of bearing pandemic risk includes the cost of the capital needed to ensure, with a given probability, that insurers have sufficient resources to finance claim payments. The planning probabilities that insurers are thought to use in making this decision are high—99 percent or higher.[1] For this analysis, we have assumed that a pandemic is a dichotomous random variable and that insurers plan for an event that is of the same magnitude as the current event. The planning loss (*ploss*) in this case is thus insurer claims plus LAE should a pandemic occur plus G&SE.

$$ploss = insurer\_claims * (1 + LAE\_ratio) . \tag{C.8}$$

In PRIA and Chubb's BEIP, the insurers retain all the premium and thus

$$capital = (1 - dindex) * (ploss - (premium - G\&SE - ror * capital)) . \tag{C.9}$$

In Pandemic Re, insurers receive only a part of the premium, which will be addressed below.

Rearranging C.9 yields

$$capital = \frac{ploss - premium + G\&SE}{\alpha} , \tag{C.10}$$

where

$$\alpha = \frac{1}{1 - dindex} - ror$$

$$0 \leq dindex < 1 .$$

Premium is the sum of expected annual loss, expected annual LAE, G&SE, and the costs of capital required to hedge solvency risk:

$$premium = event\_prob * insurer\_claims * (1 + LAE_{ratio}) + G\&SE + ror * capital, \tag{C.11}$$

where *event_prob* is the event probability used by the agent (either insurers or the government) in setting premium. Substituting C.10 into C.11 and rearranging yields the following for the PRIA program:

---

1 Dixon et al., 2007, p. 17.

$$premium_{PRIA} = G\&SE + \frac{event\_prob * insurer\_claims * (1 + LAE\_ratio) + \left(\frac{ror}{\alpha}\right) * ploss}{1 + \frac{ror}{\alpha}}. \tag{C.12}$$

Because no capital is required by the BCPP and all claims are funded by the government,[2] the premium calculation for the BCPP simplifies to

$$premium_{BCPP} = G\&SE + event\_prob * insured\_loss * (1 + LAE\_ratio). \tag{C.13}$$

Equation C.12 is also used to calculate the premium for Chubb's BEIP for small and medium-sized firms.

Insurers retain only a portion of the premium in Pandemic Re, and we assume that insurers also retain the amount needed to cover their annual G&SE:

$$premium\ retained\ by\ insurers_{PanRe} = industry\_copay * premium + (1 - industry\_copay) * G\&SE. \tag{C.14a}$$

$$premium\ ceded\ to\ govt_{PanRe} = (1 - industry\_copay) * (premium - G\&SE). \tag{C.14b}$$

We combine C.14a, C.10, and C.11 and recognize that the premium in Pandemic Re is set at a market-based rate that covers the risk borne by both the government and insurers. The premium becomes

$$premium_{PanRe} = G\&SE + \frac{event\_prob * insured\_loss * (1 + LAE\_ratio) + \left(\frac{ror}{\alpha}\right) * ploss}{1 + \frac{ror}{\alpha} * copay\_industry}. \tag{C.15}$$

The take-up rates for the Chubb and PRIA programs are calculated using a constant elasticity demand curve that has been fit to the premium and take-up rate for the BCPP. The demand curve is of the form

---

2 Insurers participating in the BCPP, as well as the other proposed programs, may face risk that the government will delay or fail to reimburse insurers for claim payments and expenses. Such risk is not considered in this analysis.

$$Q_d = \beta * \left(\frac{premium}{participating\_firms} \right)^{-k}, \tag{C.16}$$

where Q_d is the number of firms participating in the program and $-k$ is the demand elasticity. The value for the demand elasticity in the base case is –0.50, and β is determined using the projected premium per firm and assumed take-up rate for the BCPP. The demand equation is then used to project take-up for the Chubb and PRIA programs using the projected premiums for those programs. The premium and take-up rates in the Chubb and PRIA programs are adjusted using the supply relationships (C.12–C.15) and demand relationship (C.16) until the market reaches equilibrium.

APPENDIX D

General and Selling Expense and Loss Adjustment Expense Ratios by Line of Business

Table D.1 reports the G&SE for P&C insurance in the United States by line of business based on the annual statements submitted by insurers to the National Association of Insurance Commissioners. Also reported is ratio of G&SE to premium written. To smooth out annual variation in the ratio, G&SE and premium are each summed over the five-year period spanning 2015 to 2019. Table D.2 contains similar information for LAE, direct incurred losses, and the LAE ratio.

Table D.1
General and Selling Expense Ratio by Line of Business Between 2015 and 2019

Line of Business	Direct Written Premium ($1,000s)	G&SE ($1,000s)	Ratio of G&SE to Premium
Accident & health	31,814,525	7,918,434	0.249
Aircraft	8,210,399	2,138,151	0.260
Allied lines	57,707,058	16,109,499	0.279
Boiler & machinery	8,749,284	2,677,392	0.306
Burglary & theft	1,607,666	542,205	0.337
Commercial auto	179,308,672	47,045,168	0.262
Commercial multiple peril (liability)	74,977,328	23,721,032	0.316
Commercial multiple peril (nonliability)	129,430,443	39,595,324	0.306
Credit	10,140,205	3,318,878	0.327
Earthquake	11,722,601	2,998,260	0.256
Farmowners multiple peril	21,186,593	5,801,467	0.274
Federal flood	14,409,404	3,432,840	0.238
Fidelity	6,222,379	1,965,377	0.316
Financial guaranty	5,834,175	2,299,795	0.394

Table D.1—Continued

Line of Business	Direct Written Premium ($1,000s)	G&SE ($1,000s)	Ratio of G&SE to Premium
Fire	64,866,013	17,310,988	0.267
Homeowners multiple peril	466,275,407	119,320,224	0.256
Inland marine	113,496,742	30,052,156	0.265
International	339,248	289,823	0.854
Medical professional liability	46,129,920	9,666,079	0.210
Mortgage guaranty	25,292,672	5,635,553	0.223
Multiple peril crop	49,516,999	5,422,631	0.110
Ocean marine	17,728,623	4,942,283	0.279
Other P&C	7,196,874	1,758,662	0.244
General liability (other liability and product liability combined)	346,047,180	89,933,360	0.260
Personal auto	1,125,460,577	238,944,576	0.212
Private crop	5,198,145	1,191,984	0.229
Private flood	2,012,950	582,827	0.290
Surety	30,375,003	14,441,833	0.475
Warranty	12,945,324	2,345,340	0.181
Workers comp	275,414,629	57,867,280	0.210
All P&C lines	3,149,617,038	759,269,421	0.241

SOURCE: National Association of Insurance Commissioners data via S&P Global Intelligence, provided to RAND by the American Property Casualty Insurance Association.

Table D.2
Loss Adjustment Expense Ratio by Line of Business Between 2015 and 2019

Line of Business	Direct Incurred Loss ($1,000s)	LAE ($1,000s)	Ratio of LAE to Direct Incurred Loss
Accident & health	24,028,892	1,317,504	0.055
Aggregate write-ins	3,285,362	382,824	0.117
Aircraft	4,688,739	871,490	0.186
Allied lines	47,331,501	4,619,968	0.098
Boiler & machinery	3,533,629	244,793	0.069
Burglary & theft	452,303	67,444	0.149
Commercial multiple peril (liability)	36,575,534	17,014,514	0.465
Commercial multiple peril (nonliability)	77,240,461	8,464,595	0.110
Commercial auto	123,397,681	22,035,696	0.179
Credit	4,441,500	356,332	0.080
Earthquake	264,489	78,853	0.298
Farmowners multiple peril	12,593,644	1,359,583	0.108
Federal flood	15,739,579	904,611	0.057
Fidelity	2,351,748	309,658	0.132
Financial guaranty	2,694,464	828,519	0.307
Fire	36,319,805	3,210,440	0.088
Homeowners multiple peril	286,960,410	41,501,726	0.145
Inland marine	56,244,592	4,198,689	0.075
International	220,661	36,985	0.168
Medical professional liability	22,485,904	12,748,962	0.567
Mortgage guaranty	3,419,471	294,421	0.086
Multiple peril crop	34,112,439	974,899	0.029
Ocean marine	9,622,185	1,305,775	0.136
General liability (other liability and product liability combined)	202,117,172	56,944,364	0.282
Personal auto	758,526,979	127,147,169	0.168
Private crop	4,881,920	194,393	0.040
Private flood	1,431,272	64,389	0.045
Surety	4,934,434	1,511,457	0.306

Table D.2—Continued

Line of Business	Direct Incurred Loss ($1,000s)	LAE ($1,000s)	Ratio of LAE to Direct Incurred Loss
Warranty	7,469,610	303,029	0.041
Workers comp	138,269,326	36,351,867	0.263
All P&C lines	1,925,635,706	345,644,949	0.179

SOURCE: National Association of Insurance Commissioners data via S&P Global Intelligence, provided to RAND by the American Property Casualty Insurance Association.

References

American Property Casualty Insurance Association, "Property Casualty Insurance Industry Suffered Largest-Ever Drop in Surplus in the First Quarter of 2020," July 28, 2020.

American Property Casualty Insurance Association, Independent Insurance Agents and Brokers of America, Inc., and National Association of Mutual Insurance Companies, *Business Continuity Protection Program*, updated September 2020. As of May 5, 2021:
https://home.treasury.gov/system/files/311/BCPP-Overview-9-20.pdf

Autor, David, David Cho, Leland D. Crane, Mita Goldar, Byron Lutz, Joshua Montes, William B. Peterman, David Ratner, Daniel Villar, and Ahu Yildirmaz, "An Evaluation of the Paycheck Protection Program Using Administrative Payroll Microdata," unpublished manuscript, July 22, 2020. As of May 5, 2021:
https://economics.mit.edu/files/20094

Barinov, Alexander, Jianren Xu, and Steven W. Pottier, "Estimating the Cost of Equity Capital for Insurance Firms with Multiperiod Asset Pricing Models," *Journal of Risk and Insurance*, Vol. 87, No. 1, 2020, pp. 213–245.

Business Continuity Coalition, homepage, undated. As of May 10, 2021:
https://www.businesscontinuitycoalition.com

———, "BCC Proposal: A Proposal from the Policyholder Community," September 2020. As of January 19, 2021:
https://home.treasury.gov/system/files/311/FACI-BCC-Proposal-9-20.pdf

———, "Pandemic Risk Insurance Act Business Continuity Coalition Proposal: Section-by-Section Description," March 2021. As of April 16, 2021:
https://www.businesscontinuitycoalition.com/recommended-proposal

Businesswire, "Most Small Business Owners at Risk for a Disaster," August 31, 2015. As of April 4, 2021:
https://www.businesswire.com/news/home/20150831005924/en/

Cardona-Ospina, Jaime A., Valentina Henao-SanMartin, Wilmer F. Acevedo-Mendoza, Katherinn Melissa Nasner-Posso, Dayron F. Martínez-Pulgarín, Abril Restrepo-López, Valentina Valencia-Gallego, Matthew H. Collins, and Alfonso J. Rodriguez-Morales, "Fatal Zika Virus Infection in the Americas: A Systematic Review," *International Journal of Infectious Diseases*, Vol. 88, November 2019, pp. 49–59.

Centers for Better Insurance, *Terrorism Risk Insurance Act: Shifting Risk Through Terrorism Insurance Captives*, Frederick, Md., 2020. As of May 20, 2021:
https://www.betterins.org/bin/resources/TRIA/TRIA%20-%20Terrorism%20Captives%20Report.pdf

Centers for Disease Control and Prevention, National Center for Emerging and Zoonotic Infectious Disease, Division of High-Consequence Pathogens and Pathology, Viral Special Pathogens Branch, "2014–2016 Ebola Outbreak in West Africa," webpage, last reviewed March 8, 2019. As of April 16, 2021:
https://www.cdc.gov/vhf/ebola/history/2014-2016-outbreak/index.html

Centers for Disease Control and Prevention, National Center for Immunization and Respiratory Diseases, "Highly Pathogenic Asian Avian Influenza A(H5N1) Virus," webpage, last reviewed December 12, 2018. As of April 16, 2021:
https://www.cdc.gov/flu/avianflu/h5n1-virus.htm

———, "2009 H1N1 Pandemic (H1N1pdm09 Virus)," webpage, last reviewed June 11, 2019. As of April 16, 2021:
https://www.cdc.gov/flu/pandemic-resources/2009-h1n1-pandemic.html

Centers for Disease Control and Prevention, National Center for Immunization and Respiratory Diseases, Division of Viral Diseases, "Frequently Asked Questions About SARS," webpage, last reviewed May 3, 2005. As of April 16, 2021:
https://www.cdc.gov/sars/about/faq.html

Chubb, *Pandemic Business Interruption Program*, Warren, N.J., July 8, 2020. As of January 14, 2021:
https://www.chubb.com/content/dam/chubb-sites/chubb-com/us-en/about-chubb/pandemic-business-interruption-program/documents/pdf/pandemic-business-interruption-program.pdf

"The Covid-19 Tracker," *STAT*, updated May 19, 2021. As of May 19, 2021:
https://www.statnews.com/feature/coronavirus/covid-19-tracker/

Cowley, Stacy, "Despite Billions in Fees, Banks Predict Meager Profits on P.P.P. Loans," *New York Times*, October 1, 2020. As of April 7, 2021:
https://www.nytimes.com/2020/10/01/business/ppp-loans-bank-profits.html

Dalton, Michael, Elizabeth Weber Handwerker, and Mark A. Loewenstein, "Employment Changes by Employer Size During the COVID-19 Pandemic: A Look at Current Employment Statistics Survey Microdata," *Monthly Labor Review*, U.S. Bureau of Labor Statistics, October 2020.

Dixon, Lloyd, Robert J. Lempert, Tom LaTourrette, and Robert T. Reville, *The Federal Role in Terrorism Insurance: Evaluating Alternatives in an Uncertain World*, Santa Monica, Calif.: RAND Corporation, MG-679-CTRMP, 2007. As of May 5, 2021:
https://www.rand.org/pubs/monographs/MG679.html

Dixon, Lloyd, Flavia Tsang, and Gary Fitts, *The Impact of Changing Wildfire Risk on California's Residential Insurance Market*, Sacramento: California Natural Resources Agency, August 2018. As of May 5, 2021:
https://www.rand.org/pubs/external_publications/EP67670.html

Federal Insurance Office, U.S. Department of the Treasury, *Report on the Effectiveness of the Terrorism Risk Insurance Program*, Washington, D.C., June 2020.

Hartwig, Robert, Greg Niehaus, and Joseph Qiu, "Insurance for Economic Losses Caused by Pandemics," *Geneva Risk and Insurance Review*, Vol. 45, 2020, pp. 134–170.

Insurance Services Office, Businessowners Coverage Form, BP 00 03 01 10, 2009. As of April 5, 2021:
https://www.propertyinsurancecoveragelaw.com/files/file/BP%2000%2003%2001%2010.pdf

Insureon, "How Much Does a Business Owner's Policy Cost?" webpage, undated-a. As of April 5, 2021:
https://www.insureon.com/small-business-insurance/business-owners-policy/cost

———, "How Much Does Business Interruption Insurance Cost?" webpage, undated-b. As of April 5, 2021:
https://www.insureon.com/small-business-insurance/business-interruption/cost

Internal Revenue Service, *Statistics of Income—2017: Corporation Income Tax Returns*, Washington, D.C., 2020. As of February 5, 2021:
https://www.irs.gov/statistics/soi-tax-stats-corporation-complete-report

Kielholz, Walter, "The Cost of Capital for Insurance Companies," *Geneva Papers on Risk and Insurance*, Vol. 25, No. 1, January 2000, pp. 4–24.

Kunreuther, Howard, and Erwann Michel-Kerjan, *TRIA and Beyond: Terrorism Risk Financing in the U.S.*, Philadelphia: Wharton Risk Management and Decision Process Center, University of Pennsylvania, August 2005. As of February 5, 2021:
https://riskcenter.wharton.upenn.edu/wp-content/uploads/2014/07/TRIA-and-Beyond.pdf

Marsh, *2019 Terrorism Risk Insurance Report*, New York, May 2019.

Michel-Kerjan, Erwann, Paul Raschky, and Howard Kunreuther, "Corporate Demand for Insurance: New Evidence from the U.S. Terrorism and Property Markets," *Journal of Risk and Insurance*, Vol. 82, No. 3, September 2015, pp. 505–530.

National Academy of Social Insurance, *Workers' Compensation: Benefits, Coverage, and Costs*, Washington, D.C., November 2020. As of February 18, 2021:
https://www.nasi.org/sites/default/files/research/
November%202020%20-%20Benefits,%20Coverage,%20and%20Costs.pdf

National Association of Insurance Commissioners, *Report on Profitability by Line by State in 2018*, Kansas City, Mo., 2019.

National Flood Insurance Program, Federal Emergency Management Agency, *The Watermark*, Vol. 11, June 2020. As of January 22, 2021:
https://www.fema.gov/sites/default/files/2020-09/fema_watermark_report_06-2020.pdf

Pub. L. 116-136, Coronavirus Aid, Relief, and Economic Security Act, March 27, 2020.

Reed, Carrie, Matthew Biggerstaff, Lyn Finelli, Lisa M. Koonin, Denise Beauvais, Amra Uzicanin, Andrew Plummer, Joe Bresee, Stephen C. Redd, and Daniel B. Jernigan, "Novel Framework for Assessing Epidemiologic Effects of Influenza Epidemics and Pandemics," *Emerging Infectious Diseases*, Vol. 19, No. 1, January 2013, pp. 85–91.

Ribas Freitas, André Ricardo, Marcelo Napimoga, and Maria Rita Donalisio, "Assessing the Severity of COVID-19," *Epidemiologia e Serviços de Saúde*, Vol. 29, No. 2, April 2020.

U.S. Bureau of Economic Analysis, "Gross Domestic Product, Third Quarter 2020 (Advance Estimate)," webpage, last modified October 30, 2020. As of May 5, 2021:
https://www.bea.gov/news/2020/gross-domestic-product-third-quarter-2020-advance-estimate

U.S. Bureau of Labor Statistics, "Employer Costs for Employee Compensation—September 2020," December 17, 2020. As of May 5, 2021:
https://www.bls.gov/news.release/archives/ecec_12172020.htm

U.S. Census Bureau, "Number of Firms, Number of Establishments, Employment, Annual Payroll, and Preliminary Receipts by Enterprise Employment Size for the United States, All Industries: 2017," Excel file, March 6, 2020. As of May 5, 2021:
https://www.census.gov/data/tables/2017/econ/susb/2017-susb-annual.html

U.S. House of Representatives, Pandemic Risk Insurance Act of 2020, H.R. 7011, May 26, 2020.

U.S. Small Business Administration, "PPP Data: Find Data and Reports Related to the Paycheck Protection Program (PPP)," webpage, undated. As of March 29, 2021:
https://www.sba.gov/funding-programs/loans/covid-19-relief-options/paycheck-protection-program/ppp-data

———, "Second Updated Paycheck Protection Program Lender Processing Fee Payment and 1502 Reporting Process," Procedural Notice 5000-20091, February 8, 2021. As of April 7, 2021:
https://www.sba.gov/sites/default/files/2021-02/Procedural%20Notice%205000-20091%20-%202nd%20Updated%20PPP%20Processing%20Fee%20and%201502%20Reporting-508.pdf

U.S. Small Business Administration, Office of Advocacy, "A Look at Nonemployer Businesses," factsheet, August 2018. As of April 7, 2021:
https://www.sba.gov/sites/default/files/advocacy/Nonemployer-Fact-Sheet.pdf

World Health Organization, "Middle East Respiratory Syndrome Coronavirus (MERS-CoV)," webpage, undated. As of April 16, 2021:
https://www.who.int/health-topics/middle-east-respiratory-syndrome-coronavirus-mers#tab=tab_1

Zurich, *Zurich's Draft Concept for Facilitating Pandemic Protection*, Los Angeles, Calif., December 7, 2020. As of January 14, 2021:
https://www.zurichna.com/-/media/project/zwp/zna/docs/kh/pandemic/zurich-pandemic-risk-concept-powerpoint-final.pdf?la=en&hash=3E3F7670DC6B7E0523EA1D700082D7DD